Differentiating Learning Differences from Disabilities

Meeting Diverse Needs through Multi-Tiered Response to Intervention

Acquiring Editor: Virginia C. Lanigan
Editorial Assistant: Matthew Buchholz
Editor in Chief: Jeffery Johnston
Production Editor: Annette Joseph
Editorial Production Service: DB Publishing Services, Inc.
Composition Buyer: Linda Cox
Manufacturing Buyer: Megan Cochran
Interior Designer: Denise Hoffman
Cover Administrator: Linda Knowles
Cover Designer: Jenny Hart

This book was set in Minion by Denise Hoffman. It was printed and bound by Bind-Rite. The cover was printed by Phoenix Color.

Pearson Education, Ltd.   Pearson Education Australia Pty. Limited
Pearson Education Singapore Pte. Ltd   Pearson Education North Asia Ltd.
Pearson Education Canada, Ltd.   Pearson Educación de Mexico, S.A. de C.V.
Pearson Education–Japan   Pearson Education Malaysia Pte. Ltd.

Merrill
Is an Imprint of

www.pearsonhighered.com

10 9 8 7 6 5 4 3 2 1

ISBN 13: 978-0-205-60827-0
ISBN 10: 0-205-60827-2

▶ **This book is dedicated to my family:**
Robin

Joseph

Jeremy

Rachael

Forms Included in This Book

Note: All Forms are designed as informal guides to assist educators in addressing important topics, issues, and practices essential to the area to which each Form relates. Forms were developed from literature sources cited in the book as well as my educational experiences over the past several decades. All Forms were field reviewed for accuracy and clarity of content.

Contents

Preface

THE EDUCATION OF DIVERSE LEARNERS IN TODAY'S CLASSROOMS continues to challenge even the most experienced educators. Issues such as immigration, overrepresentation of diverse learners in special education, or shortages of highly qualified teachers are some of the many factors that contribute to the misidentification of learning differences as disabilities. Only through informed decision-making completed within the context of unbiased assessment and instruction will the trend of misinterpreting differences as disabilities be reversed. The overall purposes of *Differentiating Learning Differences from Disabilities: Meeting Diverse Needs through Multi-Tiered Response to Intervention* are to: (1) assist educators in providing effective education to culturally and linguistically diverse learners at-risk within multi-level response to intervention models; (2) avoid misinterpreting learning and cultural differences as learning or behavior disabilities through effective assessment and evidence-based interventions; and (3) develop skills for effective collaboration among special and general educators to meet diverse learners' needs in multi-tiered settings. These purposes are accomplished by simultaneously discussing expected and typical behaviors associated with the development of English as a second language, diverse cultural norms/values, and learning/behavior disability characteristics and needs. Readers will acquire an understanding of each of these three areas individually and in interrelated ways to help them more effectively clarify difference from disability.

This book provides practitioners with content, forms, and guides (reproducible) for educating diverse learners within multi-tiered instruction and response to intervention models. This book includes eight chapters. Chapter 1 provides an overview of learning differences and disability issues confronting diverse learners. In this chapter, various educational practices that contribute to the misidentification of learning differences as disabilities are presented along with factors to be aware of that perpetuate bias in education and assessment for diverse learners. Chapter 1 also describes a process educators may follow to become more culturally proficient teachers. Chapter 2 discusses three-tiered instruction and response to intervention including ways to make these educational practices culturally responsive. Also discussed is the problem-solving model for use in making progress-monitoring decisions. Chapter 3 provides discussion and comparison of behaviors expected during second language acquisition and various cultural values and behaviors and how these are similar to learning or behavior disorders, which can lead to the misinterpretation of learning differences as disorders.

Chapters 4 and 5 discuss a variety of assessment issues and practices put in the context of culturally responsive education. In Chapter 4, culturally valid assessment, including several cultural and linguistic factors that must be considered and accounted for in order to complete an appropriate assessment of diverse learners, is discussed. These include language function, experiential background, teaching and learning instructional styles, as well as acculturation and cultural values and norms. Chapter 4 also includes a listing of the knowledge and many skills necessary to complete a culturally valid assessment process. In Chapter 5, a variety of assessment practices are presented with specific applications to cultural and linguistic relevance for diverse learners. Also discussed are curriculum-based measurement, performance-based assessment, and assessment accommodations. Chapter 6 ties together the various concepts, practices, skills, and procedures discussed in the first five chapters to form an ecological perspective in meeting culturally responsive assessment and education in order to avoid the recurring practices that lead to misinterpretation of a learning difference as a learning disability or a behavior disorder. Chapter 7 presents a variety of evidence-based interventions for use with diverse learners. The book concludes (Chapter 8) with a discussion about the importance of collaboration among general and special educators, bilingual/ESL teachers, assessment personnel, speech and language specialists, as well as other educational personnel included on a problem-solving team. In addition, two appendices are included. Appendix A provides additional teaching interventions to support and differentiate instruction for diverse learners. Appendix B provides numerous websites that contain information related to the topics covered in this book including RTI, evidence-based interventions, curriculum-based measurement, and diversity education.

Each chapter begins with a statement of the significance of the chapter's content to today's instructional environments followed by a summary overview, key topics, and learner outcomes. Each chapter concludes with suggested additional activities to support each chapter's learner outcomes. This book was written for the many practitioners directly involved in the implementation of multi- or three-tiered instruction for at-risk culturally and linguistically diverse students struggling in the classroom. Educators who are responsible for direct and supplemental instruction, on-going progress monitoring to determine response to three-tiered evidence-based interventions as well as those included on school- or district-based problem-solving teams, will benefit from this text. It is my hope that the contents of this book provide practitioners with valuable information and resources to reduce bias, inappropriate referrals to special education, and current practices that contribute to misinterpretation of the learning needs of diverse students by making more informed decisions concerning the differentiation of learning differences from learning or behavior disorders.

JJH

Acknowledgments

I WISH TO ACKNOWLEDGE THE SERVICE AND WORK of all the educators with whom I have had and continue to have the privilege of knowing and working with over the past three decades. The challenges associated with providing effective education to culturally and linguistically diverse learners continue to require on-going professional development and growth in culturally competent teaching and assessment, in advances to improve perceptions about the value of diversity in education, and in knowledge and skills to effectively implement multi-tiered response to intervention. The dedication of these educators of diverse learners is commendable. I also wish to thank Dr. Michael Orosco for his contribution as a co-author of Chapter 3 and wish to acknowledge the field reviewers of this book: Craig Kennedy, Vanderbilt University; Colleen Klein-Ezell, Southeastern Louisiana University; Judith Mazur, Buena Vista Elementary; Donna Schweitzer, Forwood Elementary School; Patti Taillacq, Marlborough Intermediate Elementary School; and Barbara Wilmes, University of Central Arkansas.

In addition, I wish to thank the educators who reviewed and have used the different Forms in this book and provided feedback concerning their development and revisions. In particular, I was to acknowledge Ms. Amy Eppolito, doctoral candidate, University of Colorado at Boulder. The comments and suggestions from each of these educators improved the quality of this book and added valuable content to best assist educators in the teaching and assessment of diverse learners in today's schools.

CHAPTER 1

Overview of Learning Difference and Disability Issues for Diverse Learners

Significance to Contemporary Educational Contexts

CONTROVERSY OVER THE MISIDENTIFICATION and misplacement of culturally and linguistically diverse learners into special education has plagued our nation's schools for decades. Today, we see concentrated efforts from all levels of education—national, state, local—to reduce practices that facilitate the misdiagnosis of a learning difference as a learning and/or behavior disorder. Educators throughout our nation's schools are increasingly recognizing that many current practices contribute directly to misidentifying a learning difference as a learning disorder. This is highly significant in today's instructional environments because educators are actively seeking assessment and curricular strategies and procedures that improve decision-making to reduce erroneously identifying learning differences as disabilities.

▶ Overview

The complex issues associated with the controversy over misidentification and overrepresentation of diverse learners in special education are presented. Discussions include several current educational practices and situations that perpetuate the misinterpretation of a learning difference as a disability. Suggestions for reducing or eliminating the educational practices that continue to facilitate misidentification for special education of diverse learners are offered. These include the importance of a problem-solving team and the process for developing culturally competent teaching. This chapter concludes with discussions about differentiating instruction for diverse learners at-risk to assist in discerning difference from disability.

▶ Key Topics

- ▶ overrepresentation
- ▶ misidentification of educational practices
- ▶ team decision-making
- ▶ culturally proficient teaching
- ▶ differentiation

▶ Learner Outcomes

Upon completion of this chapter, the reader will be able to:

1. Articulate current issues related to cultural/linguistic diversity and overrepresentation in special education.
2. Describe general practices that facilitate overrepresenting diverse learners in special education.
3. Articulate specific tasks to complete to avoid overrepresenting diverse learners in special education.
4. Describe the importance of a team problem-solving process for making effective instructional decisions for diverse learners at-risk in education.
5. Articulate team member skills, qualities, and abilities to meet the needs of diverse learners who are at-risk in today's classrooms.
6. Evaluate culturally proficient teaching abilities.
7. Describe how the practice of differentiation assists to discern learning difference from disability.

INTRODUCTION

To begin to address the topic of differentiating learning difference and disability, several general practices seen in today's educational systems that perpetuate the overrepresentation of diverse learners in special education are explored. However, prior to these discussions, the terms used throughout this book are provided here to assist you with current and emerging terms and practices:

- *No Child Left Behind (NCLB).* Federal legislation that became law in 2001 requiring all students to meet high standards of learning, including those at-risk.

- *Individuals with Disabilities Education Improvement Act (IDEA).* The 2004 reauthorization of the major federal legislation mandating free and appropriate education for all students.

- *Evidence-Based Interventions.* Research-based interventions that demonstrate effectiveness for intended uses and designed purposes.

- *Response to Intervention (RTI).* Systematic implementation of evidence-based interventions along with on-going progress monitoring to best determine the level and intensity of instruction to provide to learners at-risk.

- *Multi-Tiered Instruction.* Levels of instruction (e.g., three-tiered instruction) provided to students that increase the evidence-based interventions in duration and intensity based on response to intervention progress-monitoring results.

- *Cultural and Linguistic Diversity.* Values, norms, and languages representing a variety of ethnicities and cultural heritages.

- *Learners At-Risk.* Students in school who struggle academically and/or behaviorally.

- *Culturally Responsive Education.* Teaching and learning that integrates and connects with students within a sociocultural context (Klingner & Edwards, 2006).

- *Progress Monitoring.* Frequent and systematic monitoring and recording of student progress toward meeting defined educational benchmarks.

- *Differentiating Instruction.* Modification of content, process, and/or product relative to individual student needs (Bender, 2002).

- *English Language Learner (ELL).* A student who is in the process of learning English (Ovando, Collier, & Combs, 2003).

- *Collaboration.* Continuous and professional exchange of knowledge, skills, and expertise among educators to identify and solve problems (Idol, Paolucci-Whitcomb, & Nevin, 1995).

language (i.e., English). In this type of scenario, concluding that the student has a learning disability because of issues while using a second language is erroneous because similar issues are not apparent when the learner uses the first language. Therefore, student abilities in academics must be determined in both languages before consideration of a disability.

■ *Lack of Instructional Emphasis on Development of Higher-Order Thinking.* A frequent misperception about diverse learners is their inability to use higher-order thinking skills in the classroom. Often, teachers assume that during the development of a second language, a student is incapable of using higher-order thinking. As a result, the curriculum is made less challenging and inhibits the further development of higher-level thinking (i.e., analysis, synthesis, evaluation). This, in turn, frequently leads to a referral for special education due to perceived poor concept thinking skills. While for some students acquiring English, use of higher-level thinking skills in English may be a challenge, Tharp (1997) found that effective teachers challenge all learners and should include use of first language if necessary to continue developing higher-order thinking skills. Only if the inability to use higher-order abilities is found to exist in both languages should a possible disability be considered (Hoover et al., 2008).

▶ **Suggestion:** Culturally competent teaching provides diverse learners with differentiated instruction to best facilitate their use of thinking strategies commensurate with their language abilities and cultural values (Lachat, 2004). Failure to accommodate these diverse needs may result in an erroneous referral and/or placement of many learners into special education. Therefore, educators must ensure that diverse learners are challenged with higher-order thinking tasks and instruction.

■ *Insufficient Opportunities to Learn.* If a learner is not provided adequate opportunities to acquire necessary knowledge and skills, it is not possible to accurately determine learning difference from disability. Opportunities to learn must include instruction that is culturally responsive to the students (Klingner & Edwards, 2006). This relates to use of appropriate materials, evidence-based interventions, and effective instructional assessment procedures as well as appropriate classroom management (Hoover & Patton, 2005a; Hoover, 2006; McLaughlin & Shepard, 1995). Decisions concerning possible learning disabilities must initially include determination that the student has had sufficient and culturally responsive opportunities to learn.

▶ **Suggestion:** Educators should continuously evaluate the opportunities they provide to all learners in the classroom. In addition, documentation of these efforts should occur if the student is a struggling learner. This documentation will serve to help assist in the decision-making process as discussions about learning differences and disabilities occur.

■ *Biased Assessment.* Concern with biased assessment when evaluating learners has existed for several decades. Bias in assessment is found in the assessment devices, the assessment process, or a combination of the two. According to Baca and Clark (1992), approximately 25 percent of bias when assessing diverse learners is found in the instruments, while 75 percent occurs in the interpretation of the results from the assessment. It is important to initially select culturally responsive assessment devices. One must pay particular attention to accurate interpretation and application of the testing results. Accurate assessment, both of the devices and the interpretive process, is fundamental to accurately determining a learning difference from a learning disability. Table 1.1, developed from content in Hoover (2008) and Wilkinson, Ortiz, and Robertson-Courtney (2004), provides an overview of considerations to reduce bias.

> ▶ **Suggestion:** Educators must ensure that they use culturally responsive assessment. To best accomplish this, questions about the assessment process and instruments should be raised to ensure they are culturally responsive. This includes use of devices that are appropriate and relevant to the needs of diverse learners as well as a team process for interpreting assessment results within a cultural/linguistic context. This helps to avoid misinterpreting the assessment results as indications of a disability when in reality it is a learning difference. Chapters 4 and 5 of this book discuss assessment of diverse learners in detail.

As stated, these ten practices are not all-inclusive yet they capture many of the current situations confronting diverse learners as erroneous decisions are often made relative to potential learning differences and learning or behavior disabilities. An understanding of these practices is critical to reversing the trend of overrepresentation of diverse learners in special education. However, acknowledging that these practices exist is only the first step in the process. The following section provides discussion and guides to assist you in self evaluating your involvement with these practices and how you may prevent these from occurring.

Evaluating the Occurrence of Effective Educational Practices

As an individual general or special educator you have the power within your own educational situation to reduce, minimize, or otherwise prevent the inappropriate educational practices previously described that frequently lead to misidentification of diverse learners for special education. Chapter 8 provides discussion and examples of collaboration and how it will assist in reducing the is a process that includes six stages, beginning with the lack of awareness or acknowledgment of cultural differences and proceeding to cultural competence and proficiency where cultural differences are valued, explored, and genuinely integrated into the curriculum. The following is a summary of the six stages as discussed by Cross et al. (1989), Gay (2000), Hoover et al. (2008), and Mason (1993):

Stage	Teaching Characteristics—Cultural differences are . . .
1. Cultural Destructiveness	Not acknowledged, viewed as problems, and are not incorporated into the curriculum
2. Cultural Incapacity	Ignored, given little (if any) attention, and cultural identity is viewed indifferently by educators in unsupportive ways in the classroom
3. Cultural Blindness	Acknowledged by educators; however, cultural differences are viewed as unimportant and as having little significance in daily curriculum and instruction
4. Cultural Precompetence	Acknowledged, valued, and of concern to educators to the extent that professional development in culturally competent teaching is undertaken; efforts are made to incorporate cultural and linguistic values into the curriculum on a regular, yet limited and sporadic basis (e.g., isolated coverage of culture and diversity)
5. Cultural Competence	Genuinely valued and incorporated into classroom instruction, activities, and dialogue on a regular integrated basis (e.g., daily examples of items, people, or significant events representing various diverse cultures)
6. Cultural Proficiency	Significantly embedded in daily teaching and learning at all levels of education

The development of cultural proficiency is a lifelong process. For many teachers, it begins formally by completing a college course in multicultural education or through field experiences in classrooms that include diverse learners. However, as previously discussed, formal and extensive exposure to multicultural education does not exist in many college and university teacher preparation programs. As a result, most teachers of diverse learners must engage in professional development activities and programs to sufficiently develop cultural proficiency in teaching as progression through these stages occurs.

Culturally responsive education requires the teacher to be in at least a later-stage 4 or preferably stages 5 to 6 in the development process. Teachers operating in this range of competence provide opportunities to best meet the various needs of diverse learners as well as feel confident in the problem-solving team's ability to discern learning difference from disability.

Differentiation of Instruction to Meet Learning Differences

Once a teacher has developed culturally competent/proficient abilities, another effective educational practice that assists in distinguishing learning differences from learning or behavior disabilities is differentiation of curriculum and instruction. The current situation in most school systems is that all learners need to be educated within mandated state or district curricula (Hoover & Patton, 2005a). This includes culturally and linguistically diverse students as well as at-risk learners. In many school districts nationwide, this mandated curriculum is standards based and is associated with statewide standards-based assessment. These mandated curricula often lack culturally responsive content and/or pedagogy and therefore contain potentially culturally biased information, teaching strategies unfamiliar to some learners, or otherwise possess expectations many culturally and linguistically diverse students are unable to meet without necessary modifications. Without needed differentiation, many diverse learners are at-risk for academic and/or social failure as they attempt to learn through these mandated curricula as their behaviors are misinterpreted as disorders rather than differences. Table 1.2, developed from content discussed by Hoover et al. (2008) and Klingner, Hoover, and Baca (2008), illustrates examples of selected behaviors associated with second language acquisition, cultural diversity, and learning/behavior disabilities. If not considered in the proper context, cultural and linguistic behaviors may be misinterpreted as learning or behavior disorders.

As shown in the table, many of the behaviors that are typical and normal based on cultural values and/or stages of second language acquisition may appear to reflect learning or behavior disorders. However, the underlying reasons for the behaviors differ significantly. Specifically, learning or behavior disabilities reflect problems or needs intrinsic to the learner; that is, the problems are a result of conditions within the student that require intensive interventions that address problems/needs within the learner. This topic is further emphasized throughout this book and more specifically discussed in Chapter 3.

competence in the classroom. An emphasis on culturally responsive education is necessary to best meet the needs of diverse learners, including more accurately discerning learning difference from learning or behavior disability.

Additional Activities to Support Learner Outcomes

1. Conduct an analysis of the extent to which culturally responsive instruction is implemented in your school.

2. Develop and implement a PowerPoint presentation for teachers to assist them to better understand the instructional and assessment needs of diverse learners.

3. Lead a child study or RTI team meeting ensuring that cultural and linguistic factors are considered in the discussions concerning a possible disability.

4. Develop with a colleague a professional development plan for further developing your cultural proficiency in teaching. Complete the professional development plan.

FORM 1.1 Guide for Determining Culturally Responsive Education

Rate the extent to which you include/emphasize the following in the classroom with diverse learners:

    1 = None (Not at all)   3 = Some (At least weekly)

    2 = Little (Once a month)   4 = Extensive (Daily)

In the *Examples* section, document two examples illustrating your skills in the area.

To what extent do you address each item in your daily instruction of diverse learners?

1. Connect with students by understanding their sociocultural environmental contexts   1 2 3 4

    Examples: A _____   B _____

2. Accommodate instruction to best reflect communication styles of students   1 2 3 4

    Examples: A _____   B _____

3. Incorporate/value diverse community practices in curriculum   1 2 3 4

    Examples: A _____   B _____

4. Adapt instruction to accommodate students' acculturation needs   1 2 3 4

    Examples: A _____   B _____

5. Develop students' linguistic competence through functional, purposeful classroom dialogue   1 2 3 4

    Examples: A _____   B _____

6. Interrelate students' prior experiences with current skills being taught (i.e., experiential background)   1 2 3 4

    Examples: A _____   B _____

7. Contextualize learning by reflecting/valuing students' native cultural values/norms into curriculum implementation   1 2 3 4

    Examples: A _____   B _____

8. Strategically engage students in on-going instructional conversation to support their interchanges and expression of ideas   1 2 3 4

    Examples: A _____   B _____

9. Provide students with cognitively challenging curriculum and instruction (i.e., emphasizing higher-order thinking)   1 2 3 4

    Examples: A _____   B _____

10. Facilitate the joint and productive completion of tasks where cooperative work and on-going verbal interactions occur   1 2 3 4

    Examples: A _____   B _____

Additional comments concerning incorporation of cultural diversity in the classroom:

CHAPTER 2

Multi-Tiered Instructional Programming and Response to Intervention for Diverse Learners

Significance to Contemporary Educational Contexts

SINCE THE EARLY 1970s, THE NUMBER OF STUDENTS identified with learning and/or behavior problems has increased significantly to a point where educators are currently questioning existing processes and procedures for identifying disabilities in struggling learners. Specifically, the current practice of waiting extended periods of time prior to providing supplemental support to at-risk learners has come under serious question. To assist in addressing these concerns, many schools have or are in the process of adopting a leveling or tiered system for providing instruction to struggling learners, including culturally and linguistically diverse students. In addition, the extent to which a student makes progress within the selected tier of intervention is regularly monitored and documented, referred to as "response to intervention." Transition to this more proactive form of instruction is significant in today's schools for culturally and linguistically diverse learners, as it has the potential to significantly reduce the misinterpretation of learning differences as learning or behavior disorders, thereby improving the education and opportunities to learn for all.

Overview

The multi-level instructional model and response to intervention are discussed as well as how educators can best meet the needs of diverse learners who are at-risk academically and/or behaviorally. Readers will learn how the practice of response to intervention within a three-tiered model can best assist educators to meet the needs of diverse learners, which ultimately assists in differentiating learning differences from disabilities. A problem-solving model for making multi-tiered response to intervention decisions is also presented.

Key Topics

- ▶ multi/three-tiered instruction
- ▶ response to intervention (RTI)
- ▶ culturally responsive response to intervention
- ▶ RTI decision-making models
- ▶ problem-solving model
- ▶ standard treatment protocol model
- ▶ data-driven decision-making
- ▶ progress monitoring

Learner Outcomes

Upon completion of this chapter, the reader will be able to:

1. Describe the major components within a multi-tiered instructional model.
2. Describe the components, strengths, and concerns with response to intervention.
3. Discuss the process of response to intervention within a multi-tiered system to educate diverse learners.
4. Articulate factors necessary to implement culturally responsive response to intervention.
5. Implement the collaborative problem-solving decision-making model to best meet the needs of diverse learners at-risk.

As discussed in Chapter 1, there has been a significant increase in diversity in our schools over the past several years. The appropriate education of diverse students has reached a critical time given the increase in mandated curricula and statewide assessments. One result of the overrepresentation of students in special education is the movement to use alternative means for prevention and intervention of learning problems, particularly in the area of reading. A current alternative framework being used in many school districts nationwide has two interrelated aspects: multi-tiered instructional programming and response to intervention. These aspects collectively provide a structure and a decision-making process for meeting the needs of struggling learners in today's schools. If implemented properly, multi-tiered instruction/response to intervention shows promise and potential for meeting at-risk diverse learners' educational needs, specifically related to the high incidence of diverse students identified with learning disabilities in reading. The implementation of this educational practice known as *response to intervention* must be understood from both an instructional and decision-making framework to best determine learning differences from disabilities.

Instructional Framework: Multi-Tiered Instruction

Multi-level instruction includes the use of several levels of intervention that increase in duration and intensity over time and are based on individual student needs (e.g., two to four tiers). Although various tiers are referred to, most research and literature discussions address multi-tiered instruction as consisting of three tiers of learning (Vaughn, 2003). Our discussions will present three tiers; however, should districts use a four-tier model, a similar process is followed as described in Figure 2.1 for a three-tier model. (A four-tiered model contains three levels of intervention prior to implementing special education, which is Tier 4.)

Three-Tiered Instruction

Figure 2.1, developed from discussions found in Klingner, Hoover, and Baca (2008), is a typical illustration of three-tiered instruction in which one tier is layered over another. Education reflecting a particular tier is based on student progress and response to the instruction provided.

Interventions are implemented with increasing intensity as the student progresses across tiers. Each of the tiers is summarized here (Hoover & Patton [2008]; Klingner, Méndez Barletta, & Hoover [2008]):

- *Tier 1: High Quality Core Instruction.* Evidence-based interventions taught within a challenging general class curriculum.
- *Tier 2: High Quality Targeted Supplemental Instruction.* Targeted, supplemental interventions provided to struggling learners who are not meeting established curricular benchmarks in Tier 1 instruction.
- *Tier 3: High Quality Intensive Intervention.* Specialized and intensive interventions provided to students who fail to make adequate progress toward established benchmarks in Tier 2 instruction. This tier may include special education services.

Although the tiers are depicted as a pyramid, it is important to keep in mind that these are levels of instruction and not necessarily a place for instruction. Thus, for example, when we refer to a student being educated within Tier 2, we are referring to the *type* of interventions implemented not the *place* the interventions are being implemented. As will be discussed, Tier 1 instruction

FIGURE 2.1   Multi-Tiered Instructional Framework

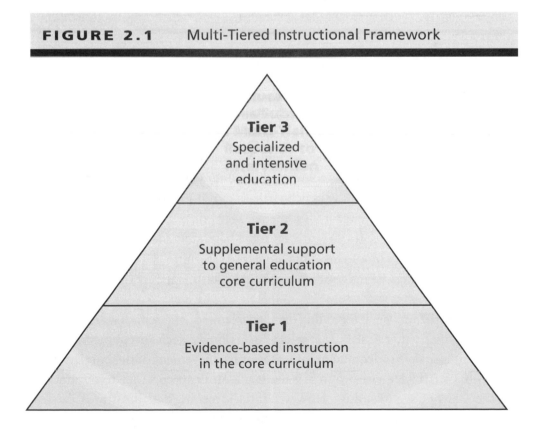

occurs in the general classroom; however, Tiers 2 and 3 interventions may also occur in the general classroom or in some other location within the school building. Although this may occur for some learners, Tiers 2 and 3 implementation of instruction does *not* automatically suggest that the student is removed from the general class setting.

A three-tiered model is designed to be preventative, countering the more traditional "wait to fail" process where a student must wait until significant problems are evident prior to receiving remediation or more targeted intervention (Brown-Chidsey & Steege, 2005). For example, in many school districts, a student must demonstrate two or more years of being below grade level prior to receiving formal remediation. In a three-tiered model of instruction, once students begin to struggle, they are provided timely intervention to address the problem before it becomes more severe. In order to be most effective, three-tiered instruction must be dynamic and not static, with instruction being implemented in integrated ways across tiers (Hoover & Patton, 2008). The following discussion addresses the general process of three-tiered instruction followed by specific considerations relevant to diverse learners.

Process of Three-Tiered Instruction

The process followed to implement three-tiered instruction is frequently presented relative to struggling readers (Vaughn, 2003), which may include many diverse learners.

TIER 1 INSTRUCTION ▪ In Tier 1, all learners in the general classroom are instructed using evidence-based interventions within a research-based curriculum. All students receive evidence-based instruction using flexible groupings and classroom structures typically found in today's general classrooms. Students in Tier 1 strive to master specific curriculum benchmarks and the same benchmarks pertain to all learners, including diverse students and those at-risk. Progress toward achieving the benchmarks is monitored on a consistent basis throughout the school year for all students. Many districts conduct this monitoring of progress three times per year: at the beginning, near the middle, and near the end of the school year. This "universal screening" serves as the initial basis for making decisions concerning progress with Tier 1 instruction for all learners.

Using the universal screening data, problem-solving school teams (e.g., Child Study, Teacher Assistance, or RTI Teams) make decisions about whether a student is making adequate progress toward achievement of the curriculum benchmarks. If adequate progress is made, the students continue to be educated in the Tier 1 core curriculum. However, if the screening data illustrate that students are making inadequate progress toward meeting the benchmarks (e.g., falling at or below the 25th percentile), those students are determined to need targeted, supplemental Tier 2 instruction. Yell (2004) estimated that approximately 80 to 90 percent of all learners are successful with Tier 1 core instruction without the need for Tier 2 or 3 intervention.

TIER 2 INTERVENTION ■ Based on Tier 1 screening showing lack of progress toward benchmarks, some learners may be considered at-risk. Students requiring Tier 2 support will demonstrate more pronounced learning needs that require targeted intervention along with Tier 1 core instruction. Tier 2 students require differentiation of instruction and/or use of more targeted interventions. Tier 2 instruction may be implemented in various settings including small homogenous groups of students implemented in the general classroom for a predetermined time period (e.g., twenty minutes daily of small-group reading support). As discussed, Tier 2 intervention begins immediately after the learner demonstrates inadequate progress in Tier 1.

Various educators (e.g., general class teacher, bilingual/ESL, reading specialist) may implement Tier 2 interventions and monitor progress more frequently (e.g., monthly). Similar to Tier 1, should Tier 2 progress monitoring demonstrate adequate progress toward benchmarks, the learner is returned to Tier 1 core instruction. However, should the learner make insufficient progress, the learner continues to receive Tier 2 supplemental support for an additional period of time to provide opportunity to make adequate progress toward meeting required benchmarks. If after a minimum of two rounds of Tier 2 interventions, learners who continue to make inadequate progress toward benchmarks are considered for more intensive Tier 3 interventions, which may include special education. In regard to the estimates, Yell (2004) wrote that between 15 to 20 percent of all learners require Tier 2 supplemental intervention sometime during their education.

TIER 3 INTERVENTION ■ Learners educated through Tier 3 have more significant educational needs in addition to not making adequate progress in Tier 2. These students need sustained intensive interventions implemented individually or in pairs or small groups. Similar to Tier 2 support, the specialized and intensive interventions in Tier 3 are completed for a defined period of time (e.g., twice per day for twelve to fifteen weeks). On-going monitoring of progress occurs very frequently (e.g., weekly). Students requiring Tier 3 interventions represent a highly select group demonstrating more significant needs that are not met in either Tier 1 or 2 instruction. Those learners who make sufficient progress with intensive interventions, based on the progress-monitoring data, are moved back into Tier 2 or possibly Tier 1. Also, as suggested, learners in Tier 3 may require formal special education assessment and/or placement. In this instance all three-tiered interventions become prereferral interventions to be used in the special education decision-making process. The prereferral issue and three-tiered instruction is discussed in more detail in a subsequent section of gathered using rigorous assessment procedures, data-driven decision-making is only effective for diverse learners if the data gathered reflect culturally responsive interventions and associated progress monitoring.

The prevailing thought is that when these three elements (i.e., evidence-based interventions, on-going progress monitoring, data-driven decisions) are implemented properly and in ways they have been designed, the decision-making process concerning tier of intervention and intensity of support is more accurate than if these elements are not included. Once appropriate interventions are selected and implemented and progress-monitoring data are gathered the task of making informed decisions challenges RTI teams responsible for the education of the students.

Response to Intervention (RTI) Decision-Making Models

Decisions concerning which tier of intervention a learner should receive are based on the student's responses to the interventions attempted as evidenced by the progress-monitoring data (Fuchs & Fuchs, 2006; Hoover & Patton, 2008). As a result, RTI decision-making is central to effective implementation of multi-tiered instruction. In regard to special education, progression through the tiers of instruction may eventually lead to a decision to refer and/or place a student into special education, particularly for learning disabilities (Bender & Shores, 2007; Fuchs, 2003). The components within the practice of RTI and associated multi-tiered instruction have been briefly discussed here and in more detail in other literature (Fuchs & Fuchs, 2006; Haager, Klingner, & Vaughn, 2007; Jimerson, Burns, & VanDerHeyden, 2007; Vaughn, 2003; Vaughn, Linan-Thompson, & Hickman, 2003; Wright, 2007). I refer the reader to those sources for more comprehensive coverage of the history and current perspectives about these topics in education.

In regard to suggested approaches for making RTI decisions, Fuchs et al. (2003) discussed the *problem-solving approach* and *standard treatment protocol approach*. Each approach addresses the RTI decision-making process in different ways.

- *Problem-Solving Approach.* This approach emphasizes a procedure that is more conducive to meeting individual needs through a process that includes preliminary identification and analysis followed by planning implementation and analysis. This approach is less rigorous than the standard treatment protocol approach; however, this approach helps to ensure that "all children with special needs receive appropriate services" (Fuchs & Fuchs, 2006, p. 97). The concern with this approach is the possibility of incorrectly identifying students as having special needs.

- *Standard Treatment Protocol Approach.* Through this approach, the use of the same intervention is emphasized for all students with similar needs (e.g., reading fluency problems). This approach is considered more accurate in identifying "children truly in need of special services" (Fuchs & Fuchs, 2006, p. 97).

While both assessment approaches may differ conceptually and operationally (Fuchs et al., 2003), they each provide a process for determining learner response to instruction. In addition, if used in combination they will emphasize both prevention and identification.

- *Combined Approach to Meet Diverse Needs.* This approach emphasizes a collaborative problem-solving process that blends the strengths of each approach to best meet the needs of all learners (McCook, 2006) (i.e., preventative process along with implementation of empirically validated interventions). Given the wide variety of experiences, backgrounds, culture, languages, and other related ecological factors seen in today's schools, the combined approach provides the best opportunity for learners at-risk, academically and/or behaviorally, to succeed with RTI. Discussed later is a five-step process (Deno, 2005) that reflects one model to use to facilitate an effective preventative-identification, problem-solving decision-making approach. Elements from both the problem-solving and standard protocol approaches can easily be incorporated into the model process discussed in the next section. The model reflects components found in various team approaches for making RTI and multi-tier educational decisions (Marston et al., 2007). The model was selected as an illustration of one decision-making process that has the potential to address many of the inappropriate educational practices discussed in Chapter 1, which in turn may facilitate discerning learning differences from disabilities more effectively.

Problem-Solving Model

The model includes five interrelated stages that assist RTI problem-solving teams to best use progress-monitoring data as well as other related and necessary information to make informed and culturally responsive decisions concerning the education of diverse learners. The five stages, developed from information found in Brown-Chidsey and Steele (2005) and Deno (2005), are illustrated in Figure 2.2 and are described here.

FORM 2.1   Evaluating Diverse Learner Considerations in the Problem-Solving Model

Instructions: Document the extent to which your problem-solving team considers each item.

1 = No Discussion   3 = Discussed to Some Extent
2 = Very Little Discussion   4 = Extensively Discussed

To what extent does the problem-solving team consider the following?

1. Cultural and linguistic factors to explain the suspected area of need	1	2	3	4
2. Gathering of sufficient supporting documentation to more clearly identify the suspected problem	1	2	3	4
3. Utilizing the following to assist in clarifying the problem:				
Classroom performance data	1	2	3	4
Charted progress-monitoring results over time	1	2	3	4
Work sample analysis	1	2	3	4
Classroom observations	1	2	3	4
Interviews	1	2	3	4
Language proficiency assessment results	1	2	3	4
4. Documented evidence that the Tier 1 instruction is culturally responsive	1	2	3	4
5. Use of culturally responsive evidence-based interventions in each tier of instruction	1	2	3	4
6. Progress-monitoring procedures being culturally responsive for the learner	1	2	3	4
7. Potential for misinterpreting a learning difference as a learning or behavior disorder	1	2	3	4
8. All evidence-based interventions are implemented in culturally responsive ways prior to moving a learner into a more intensive tier of instruction (e.g., Tier 1 to 2)	1	2	3	4
9. The teacher implementing the tiered interventions possesses culturally competent teaching abilities	1	2	3	4
10. Bias was reduced or eliminated in the tiered instruction and associated progress monitoring	1	2	3	4

Summary of extent to which the problem-solving team was culturally responsive:

CHAPTER 3

Characteristics of Second Language Acquisition, Cultural Diversity, and Learning/Behavior Disabilities

Michael Orosco AND John J. Hoover

▶ Significance to Contemporary Educational Contexts

FUNDAMENTAL TO ACCURATELY DIFFERENTIATING LEARNING DIFFERENCES from academic or behavior disorders is a working knowledge of the major learning/behavior characteristics reflective of second language acquisition, diverse cultural values and norms, as well as learning disabilities and behavioral disorders. Diverse learners exhibit expected behaviors as they acquire a second language (e.g., English) and/or adapt to a new cultural environment (e.g., school or classroom). These selected behaviors may appear similar to those typically associated with intrinsic learning or behavior disorders. This is significant in today's schools in that the implementation of multi-tiered learning and response to intervention must assist educators to better clarify linguistic and culturally appropriate behaviors to avoid the continuation of misinterpreting these behaviors as disability characteristics. Only by understanding all three areas (linguistic differences, cultural diversity, and disabilities) can educators make informed decisions concerning the needs of diverse learners.

▶ Overview

The typical and expected behaviors and characteristics associated with acquiring English as a second language and those associated with various cultural norms are discussed. We then present learning and behavior characteristics associated with learning and behavior disorders. The chapter concludes by comparing and contrasting cultural and linguistic behaviors with those of disabilities to best reduce misinterpreting learning differences as disabilities.

▶ Key Topics

- ▶ second language acquisition
- ▶ interlanguage
- ▶ code switching
- ▶ cultural diversity
- ▶ learning disabilities
- ▶ behavior disorders

▶ Learner Outcomes

Upon completion of this chapter, the reader will be able to:

1. Articulate the process of acquiring English as a second language.
2. Identify learning behaviors typically exhibited within the main stages of second language acquisition.
3. Describe cultural diversity in today's classrooms including behaviors, values, and norms.
4. Describe behaviors and characteristics typically associated with learning disabilities and behavior disorders.
5. Compare and contrast cultural/linguistic behaviors with those associated with learning and behavior disabilities.

INTRODUCTION

The basic premise of the No Child Left Behind Act (NCLB) (2001) is that student achievement in public schools must improve for all including diverse learners and students with disabilities. However, there are significant challenges confronting diverse learners in the high-stakes assessment era because these students continue to be misdiagnosed as having a disability. The fact that these students continue to be misidentified for special education is evidence that there needs to be a clearer understanding of the differences between a disability and cultural/linguistic diversity prior to referral and/or placement into special education. The literature on this topic indicates that despite the continued growth in the number of diverse learners, most schools are inadequately prepared to address their needs. As discussed in Chapter 1, a most significant challenge in addressing learning or behavior disabilities is distinguishing between second language acquisition and cultural diversity and disabilities. To best make these distinctions, an understanding and comparison of second language development, diverse cultural values, as well as disability characteristics is necessary.

Characteristics of Second Language Acquisition, Cultural Diversity, and Disabilities

The complexity of deciphering between the inherent characteristics associated with cultural and linguistic needs and a learning or behavior disability can become quite challenging when the question of whether a diverse learner has a disability arises. We begin by providing an overview of second language acquisition with specific emphasis placed on the behaviors typically expected as a learner is progressing through various stages of language acquisition. This is followed by a discussion of cultural diversity and various behaviors reflecting different values and norms. Specific behaviors often associated with learning disabilities and behavior disorders are then presented.

Second Language Acquisition

Second language acquisition is a process that is influence by several cognitive and environmental factors (Cummins, 2000; Hamayan & Damico, 1991). These include:

- *Age.* Children who begin the process of learning English as a second language during their early childhood years generally achieve higher levels of proficiency (Krashen, Long, & Scarcella, 1979).
- *Acculturation.* Patterns of second language use will take learners longer to internalize over the more outward aspects of a new culture (e.g., clothing styles, music) (Ovando, Collier, & Combs, 2003).
- *Attitude and Motivation.* A postive attitude along with high levels of motivation are important aspects necessary to achieve proficiency in a second lanaguage (Hamayan & Damico, 1991).
- *Learning Style.* A learner's culturally influenced preferred styles of learning may differ from the teacher's preferred styles of teaching, resulting in an inadeqate learning progress (Grossman, 1995), including progress toward learning a second language.

- *Native Language Proficiency.* Proficiency in the student's first language provides the foundation for successfully acquiring a second language (Coyne, Kame'enui, & Carnine, 2007; Cummins, 1989).
- *Community/Family.* Cultural and linguistic values and abilities are essential to successful second language acquistion (Baca & Cervantes, 2004).

These and related ecological factors are not all-inclusive and others apply. However, at a minimum, these need to be considered in the overall process of second language acquisition. It is beyond the scope of this book nor its purpose to provide detailed discussion about the development of a second language and the reader is referred to Cummins (2000), Ovando, Collier, and Combs (2003), and Hamayan and Damico (1991) for comprehensive coverage of this topic. Rather, we are attempting to identify expected behaviors often associated with the development of a second language (and misinterpreted as a disability), acknowledging that various cognitive and environmental factors influence this development.

Therefore, of significant concern to educators is the need to recognize that behaviors, which appear to be related to a disorder, are in fact expected and typical based on the learner's stage or level of second language acquisition. The following discussion addresses some of these primary learning behaviors associated with defined stages of second language acquisition (Baca & Cervantes, 2004; Cummins, 2000; Grossman, 1995; Hoover et al., 2008; Ovando, Collier & Combs, 2003).

- *Stage 1: Silent.* This is an active listening stage during which little English may be spoken and the learner relies on simple yes/no-type responses and on nonverbal communication. The learner, during the silent stage, may experience confusion with locus of control, poor attention, and exhibit shy or withdrawn behaviors.
- *Stage 2: Production.* During the second stage of development, the student "produces" language on a regular basis. Students in this stage generally begin with 1,000 or so words that they use and understand and further develop up to 3,000 words. Verbal expression contains short phrases or simple sentences. Initially, students may experience frustration and make grammatical errors.
- *Stage 3: Intermediate.* At this stage of second language development, a learner understands and uses approximately 6,000 words. The student begins to approach age-appropriate language use and is capable of generating complex sentences and providing opinions. Written language becomes more efficient; however, the learner in this stage may continue to make periodic errors in speech, reading, and/or writing (e.g., syntax, grammar, vocabulary, punctuation).

- *Stage 4: Advanced.* During the advanced stage, the learner is further developing and refining second language skills and abilities generally commensurate with age. Language uses, fluency, and written language skills are similar to age-level peers. Expressive and receptive language comprehension is also at an advanced level with few errors being made in using the second language.

In addition to these behaviors and learning characteristics, two specific patterns of second language usage must be understood and recognized to best differentiate learning difference from disability. These are *interlanguage* and *code switching.*

- *Interlanguage.* As students acquire a second language, they access their internal language system, which includes features such as English language rules, native language rules, and various universal language aspects common to many languages (Hamayan & Damico, 1991; Ovando, Collier, & Combs, 2003). These authors wrote further that these interlanguage characteristics may initially result in the use of English not reflective of native English speakers. This may include deviations from the standard word order in English, improper grammar usage, or other evidences of confusion with more complex sentence and grammar structures. Two important ideas must be understood to best serve learners acquiring a second language and to avoid misdiagnosis of a disability: The development of interlanguage follows a natural and systematic process and is not mastered easily or quickly, and as learners progress through the stages of acquisition their errors and confusion with various aspects of the second language are reduced, resulting in mastery of the second language over time (Ovando, Collier, & Combs, 2003). As a result, behaviors associated with normal interlanguage development must not be misinterpreted as cognitive deficits or evidence of emotional disorders.
- *Code Switching.* Another set of behaviors that reflect the complex systems associated with acquiring and using a second language is the practice of code switching. Code switching occurs as speakers shift across different grammatical structures, such as beginning a sentence using words in English while ending that same sentence with words from another language (e.g., French, Spanish, Hmong) (Hamayan & Damico, 1991). According to Ovando, Collier, and Combs (2003), code switching is both predicable and useful in the overall communication where second language acquisition is involved. Code switching is often misinterpreted as a deficit in language development or usage, rather than as the useful and higher-level language skill it is in communication.

The learners' experiences, what they are exposed to, and the opportunities for learning and development play a critical role in acquiring a second language.

Knowledge of behaviors associated with the various stages of second language development along with interlanguage and code-switching abilities provide a solid foundation for problem-solving teams to avoid misrepresenting typical, normal, and expected language errors or problems commonly found within the second language development process, as language disorders.

Cultural Diversity

Interrelated with second language acquisition needs, behaviors, and characteristics are the many values, norms, customs, and behaviors associated with cultural diversity. Challenges face learners as they attempt to adjust to a new culture, creating situations in which misinterpretation of culturally valued behaviors are seen by educators as learning or behavior disorders. In addition to language, many factors reflect diverse cultural experiences of learners such as learning styles; previous educational experiences; or family/community views toward education, respect, time, belongings, and individual achievement (Grossman, 1995; Hoover & Collier, 1985). Differentiating behavior differences from disorders requires educators to understand the learners' cultures and how those cultures teach and view different behaviors. It is not possible, nor productive, to identify all diverse behaviors that are frequently misdiagnosed as disorders; rather, some typical examples are presented in Baca and Cervantes (2004), Grossman (1995), Hoover et al. (2008), Hoover and Collier (1985), and Winzer and Mazurek (1998). These examples are not all-inclusive and are presented to emphasize the critical importance of knowing the cultures within which you teach prior to making judgments concerning a possible disability.

COOPERATIVE VERSUS COMPETITIVE LEARNING ■ "Cultures differ in the degree to which they stress cooperation, competition, and individualism" (Grossman, 1995, p. 324). In some cultures, cooperatively sharing information is encouraged and supported. In schools, this may be misinterpreted as copying or cheating (Smith, 1991). Conversely, some cultures teach children to be self-reliant, when completing work and solving problems (Grossman, 1995). This should not be misinterpreted as an inability to work with others or as conflict-generating behaviors. Within many cultures, however, cooperative learning is preferred over competitive learning which, for many students, presents significant problems should the classroom instruction be independent and competitive based. Knowing a diverse learner's cultural views toward cooperative versus competitive learning is essential to avoid misinterpreting such behaviors as indifferent, avoidance, or lazy (Winzer & Mazurek, 1998).

ACTIVE AND PASSIVE LEARNING ■ In addition to issues of cooperative and competitive learning, cultures vary on how they prefer to emphasize active and passive learning (Grossman, 1995). Students who prefer passive learning are taught to sit quietly, be attentive, and respond verbally only when asked or called upon in the classroom. Educators who prefer a more active posture in learning may misinterpret these behaviors as shyness, laziness, or emotionally based insecurity to an extreme. Although "active participatory learning has proven to be more effective than passive learning for most students" (Grossman, 1995, p. 312), not all students come to school ready for active learning and must be taught this way of education. These preferences for learning also include cultural values pertaining to the extent that learning should be teacher or student directed. A learner's inability to assume active learning in school should not automatically be considered a problem, and must be considered relative to the cultural values of that student.

MOTIVATION ■ The extent to which a student is motivated to learn also has underpinnings in cultural values and norms. For example, how the home supports learning is one of the key elements to motivation (Winzer & Mazurek, 1998). If a culture teaches that certain fields of study or careers are more male or female specific, then motivation to succeed with different subjects may be culturally based. The cultural backgrounds of students provide a foundation for shaping how students view various aspects of education, and the importance of these must be known prior to considering lack of motivation as a characteristic of a disability rather than cultural preference.

AGGRESSION ■ Behaviors typically associated with aggression (e.g., defending oneself, strong verbal expression of views) may be encouraged and taught in different cultures (Nazarro, 1981). Tolerance of aggressive behaviors may vary across cultures, and educators must be familiar with cultural expectations concerning aggression prior to labeling it as a behavior disorder. In addition, students new to U.S. school settings may be unfamiliar with acceptable behaviors, which in some instances are more restrictive to the student than in previous settings or cultural preferences (Hoover & Collier, 1985). It is important to note that aggressive behavior that is hurtful or harmful to others is not to be tolerated; rather, culturally based aggression often becomes an issue for educators, not when it is hurtful, but when it becomes more assertive than typically preferred by the teacher. However, this more assertive behavior is not to be misinterpreted as a disorder if the student is behaving in a culturally taught manner.

LOCUS OF CONTROL ■ Locus of control refers to the extent to which learners perceive whether they are controlled by internal or external forces (Hallahan et al., 2005). Student perceptions of locus of control vary significantly across cultures (Grossman, 1995). In some cultures, students believe that certain events (e.g., success, control over one's own future, responsibility for certain things) are out of one's control. This *external* locus of control perception drives how and to what extent various life tasks are undertaken. In other cultures a more *internal* locus of control (i.e., in charge of one's own efforts, future) prevails, which in turn drives task completion and views toward achievement of goals (Hoover & Collier, 2004). Although many educators strive to assist learners to achieve internal locus of control, for many diverse learners external locus of control is a cultural value and/or a temporary expected result as students adjust to new cultural environments (i.e., acculturation), and should not be viewed as a disorder.

ACCULTURATION ■ In addition to acculturation affecting the process of second language acquisition, it has specific implications when considering a diverse learner for a suspected behavior disorder. Diverse learners who are acculturating to a new educational environment may find this experience highly stressful and difficult to manage (Hoover & Collier, 2004). The stress and confusion often associated with acculturation may be evident in several behaviors considered disruptive in school, including withdrawal, aggressive acting out, distractibility, or confusion with locus of control. Educators must consider potential behavior problems relative to the acculturation levels diverse learners are experiencing. As learners become more acculturated to the school and learning environment, the side-effect behaviors of acculturation will diminish, clearly indicating the lack of a behavior disorder.

TEACHING/LEARNING STYLE COMPATIBILITY ■ A student's consistent preferences and patterns used to complete learning tasks reflect learning styles (Winzer & Mazurek, 1998). Diverse learners often experience difficulty with instruction "because their learning and behavior styles do not match their teachers' instructional styles" (Grossman, 1995, p. 139). All too often, we see learners considered for special education due to their inability to learn or behave, presumably because of some deficit; in reality, the suspected problem is a result of incompatibility between teaching style and learning style. Prior to moving ahead with any formal consideration of suspected academic or behavior problems as disabilities, the teaching and learning style compatibility should be identified. Determination of a learning difference or a disability must be grounded in the knowledge that compatible teaching–learning styles prevail, providing the student with culturally responsive education and sufficient opportunities based on cultural values and linguistic needs. The following section describes five cognitive learning styles frequently discussed in the literature for diverse learners (Baca & Cervantes, 2004; Hoover & Collier, 2003; Winzer & Mazurek, 1998). Comparison of teacher instructional styles and students' preferred styles of learning is facilitated in several guides included in this section.

COGNITIVE LEARNING STYLES ■ The manner in which a student organizes and processes information reflects one's cognitive learning style (Winzer & Mazurek, 1998). Consideration of cognitive styles is particularly relevant to diverse learners as research suggests that "there is a link between cultural background and approaches to learning" (Ovando, Collier, & Combs, 2003, p. 215). A variety of cognitive learning styles exist and it is beyond the scope of this book to provide detailed coverage of each style. For our purposes, we need to understand that cultural background influences preferred cognitive styles and that these preferences must be accommodated to provide culturally responsive education and compatible teaching instruction. Five cognitive learning styles exhibited by diverse learners follow, which may be reflective of cultural norms; styles that may be evident in the classroom that should not be misinterpreted as disorders if they differ from preferred instructional styles. These include:

1. *Field Dependent-Independent Styles.* Field-dependent learners prefer to view a pattern in its entirety rather than constituent parts. They have difficulty focusing on individual aspects or parts of a pattern or task. Field-independent learners have the ability to separate parts from the whole and attend to individual details (Winzer & Mazurek, 1998).

2. *Tempo-Reflective/Impulsive Styles.* Learners who spend time thinking through and analyzing an issue or topic prior to generating a response are demonstrating a reflective tempo or style. Those who are more spontaneous and immediate in their response to tasks or issues demonstrate an impulsive cognitive learning style (Grossman, 1995).

3. *High-Low Tolerance Styles.* A learner who prefers situations to be highly structured and consistent with little change in routine reflects a low tolerant cognitive style. Those who are highly flexible, prefer variation, and who may experience problems with rigid structure demonstrate a preference toward a highly tolerant cognitive style (McLaughlin, 1985).

4. *Broad-Narrow Categorization Styles.* Learners who emphasize inclusion of most ideas, topics, or issues in completion of tasks are considered broad categorizers. These students tend to group or cluster both primary and secondary items minimizing the possibility of omitting something important or significant. In contrast, a narrow categorizer is much more selective in what to include or exclude in a task or assignment. Students who prefer a narrow categorization style are highly detailed and exclusive in how they approach tasks, and tend to only identify the most important purpose of the assignment (Hoover & Collier, 2003; McLaughlin, 1985).

5. *High-Low Persistence Styles.* Highly persistent learners are very focused and determined to complete a task or solve a problem. These learners do not give up until they have resolved whatever it is they are working on or attempting to complete. A low persistent style is characterized by giving up easily, frequent distractions, and have difficulty remaining on-task. These learners rely heavily on skimming and scanning abilities, avoiding significant attention to detail, and desiring frequent changes (Hoover & Collier, 2003).

As one can see, learners approach tasks and problem-solving situations along a continuum relative to each cognitive learning style. Educators should be aware of these different preferred cognitive learning styles and consider them relative to teacher instructional styles. Particular cognitive learning styles may differ from typically accepted or preferred classroom practices. However, for diverse learners these may reflect cultural norms, acculturation, or second language acquisition needs and should not be misinterpreted as disorders. Low persistence or a highly reflective style may more accurately indicate a learner's stage of second language acquisition or acculturation level rather than any indication of a learning or behavioral disability. Forms 3.1 through 3.11, developed from content found in the sources previously cited for each learning style as well as Good and Brophy (1995) and Woolfolk (2006), provide opportunities for educators to record their perceptions concerning preferred instructional styles, as well as how they perceive the learner's preferred styles. These guides are designed so that educators can better understand the classroom and instructional preferences for struggling learners. They should be used along with other formal and informal assessment devices and practices. For additional information about instructional and cognitive styles, the reader is referred to Grossman (1995), Hoover and Collier (2003), Ovando, Collier, and Combs (2003), Winzer and Mazurek (1998), and Woolfolk (2006).

NONVERBAL COMMUNICATION ■ Much of our communication involves nonverbal elements such as gestures, body language, eye contact, facial expressions, or use of personal space (Winzer & Mazurek, 1998). Nonverbal communication is culturally based and, according to Nieto (1996), educators often fail to recognize nonverbal cues associated with different cultures. Nonverbal communication exhibited in the classroom by students may deviate from expected nonverbal communication behaviors. This is often reflective of cultural norms and values and should not be viewed as a learning disorder.

TIME AND SPACE CONCEPTS ■ The concepts of time and space vary across cultures (Hoover & Collier, 2004). *Time* for some cultures is highly structured with a reality of its own. For others, time is less structured, less linear, and more reflective of life events and needs, and less on a clock (Winzer & Mazurek, 1998). In regard to personal space, different cultures emphasize the use of space in various ways (e.g., more or less space; close proximity; greater social distances) (Shade & New, 1993).

If learners come from a different cultural or linguistic background these behaviors and characteristics are often either misunderstood and/or viewed as a deficit in the context of American schooling rather than as values reflecting diversity. It creates behavioral, cultural, and linguistic dissonance that appears similar to characteristics of a learning or behavior disorder. Learners may show poor motivation, engagement, or time management that reflect their cultural values toward these constructs. These learners may also have difficulty in changing activities and experience confusion with time and space movement (e.g., moving from one class period to another) due to the lack of familiarity with the educational expectations. Current research evidence cited earlier indicates that these types of cultural, linguistic, and environment factors are often misunderstood and account for misdiagnosing learning or behavior disorders.

Disabilities

As suggested, for some educators the cultural and linguistic behaviors and characteristics previously discussed are often misinterpreted as one and the same as learning or behavior disorders, due to lack of understanding of diverse cultural values and norms. To assist in determining the difference between a disorder and a difference, characteristics of learning and behavior disabilities are discussed followed by a comparison of all three behaviors (i.e., second language, cultural, disability) to best differentiate difference from disability.

LEARNING DISABILITIES (LD) ▪ Historically, a number of inherent factors have contributed to classifying learning disabilities, including the concept that LD involves intrinsic, biologically based, learning difficulties (i.e., as opposed to learning failures associated with culture, language, and socioeconomic variables), as well as specific cognitive deficits or set of deficits (i.e., as opposed to generalized learning difficulties due to differences across cultures and languages).

Various definitions of a learning disability exist with each having its strengths and weaknesses. An accepted operational definition of learning disabilities best serves our interests related to discussions in this book and is as follows: *Students with learning disabilities exhibit learning and cognitive disorders that are intrinsic to the learner* (Bradley, Danielson, & Hallahan, 2002), and are reflected in academic achievement deficits. Characteristics often associated with learning disabilities include one or more of the following along with the academic deficit (Hallahan et al., 2005):

Attention deficits. Problems maintaining attention to and remaining on tasks

Impulsivity. Tendency to respond quickly, leading to frequent errors

Hyperactivity. Persistent pattern of and inappropriate degrees of excessive movement (Cohen, Spenciner, & Twitchell, 2003)

Information-Processing Deficits (e.g., memory, perception, thinking). Problems with long- or short-term memory, perceiving and processing information, using problem-solving abilities, and regulating and adjusting one's performance as needed

While not all characteristics are found in all students with learning disabilities, these are presented so that problem-solving teams can understand potential similarities in behaviors often associated with learning disabilities and those reflective of educational needs of learners resulting from cultural and linguistic diversity.

In summary, a learner is identified as having a learning disability when he or she exhibits significant cognitive (i.e., information-processing) needs along with academic needs (e.g., lack of response to interventions) that are due to factors within (or intrinsic to) the learner and not a result of cultural/linguistic diversity or other established disabilities (e.g., emotional/behavioral disorders, physical or sensory disabilities).

BEHAVIOR DISORDERS ■ As discussed in the previous section, many student behaviors consistent with diverse cultural norms, teachings, and expectations are misunderstood or misinterpreted by educators, resulting in a misdiagnosis of a behavior problem or disorder. Similar to learning disabilities, various definitions of behavior disorders exist and each has its critics. Also, similar to the LD definition, professional organizations have generated operational definitions of behavior disorders to best serve educators and their students. An operational definition of this type best serves our discussions. The Mental Health Special Education Coalition, formed in 1987, generated the following: Students with behavior disorders exhibit "behavioral and emotional responses in school programs so different from appropriate age, cultural or ethnic norms that the responses adversely affect educational performance, including academic, social, vocational or personal skills" (Fiedler, 2003). This operational definition further emphasizes that if the exhibited problems are temporary or expected responses to stressful events in the environment are manageable with routine interventions, they are not considered behavior disorders.

Specific characteristics often associated with behavior disorders are:

1. Problems are exhibited over an extended period of time
2. Behavior is consistently seen in at least two different settings, one of which is in school
3. Learner is unresponsive to direct interventions

In summary, to be identified with a behavior disorder the learner must exhibit significant and pervasive behaviors that adversely affect various aspects of the student's life, demonstrating more serious emotional needs that vary significantly from age-related peers. Form 3.12, developed from content in the sources cited in this chapter, is a guide to document efforts to ensure that learning and social-emotional behaviors are considered within a cultural/linguistic context.

Interpreting Second Language, Culture Diversity, and Disability Behaviors

As indicated in the title of this book, the primary learner outcome is to be able to more effectively and efficiently differentiate learning differences from learning or behavior disorders. For educators of diverse learners this has become a tremendous challenge over the years due to the fact that many normal and typical behaviors associated with various facets of cultural and linguistic diversity are similar to behaviors typically exhibited by those who truly have a learning disability or behavior disorder. In the previous sections of this chapter, we have discussed behaviors often associated with:

1. acquisition of a second language (i.e., English)
2. culturally diverse values, norms, teachings, and expectations
3. learning and behavioral disabilities

The similarity among behaviors reflecting these three aspects was initially presented in Table 1.2. We conclude this chapter by reiterating the reality that similarities among these behaviors can lead to misinterpretations between difference and disabilities.

Diverse learners who exhibit behaviors or characteristics similar to that of a disability do so for reasons that reflect external situations; that is, the process of acquiring a second language or the need to adjust to a new cultural environment. However, most diverse learners who exhibit these behaviors do not exhibit them because of intrinsic conditions or disorders that interfere with their learning. These learners may require supplemental support to address the behaviors exhibited and may need extra time to adjust to new learning situations. However, this is in contrast to education for a learner with a disability, which emphasizes helping the student remediate or compensate for internal deficits, learning or emotional.

Therefore, if the learner's behaviors can be associated with his or her cultural values/norms or with stages of second language acquisition, and not with an internal problem or deficit then a learning or behavior disability is not evident. Only if the particular learning or behavior need can be linked to an intrinsic disorder can a disability be appropriately considered. Problem-solving teams must make certain that diverse learners' behaviors are a result of intrinsic needs and not a result of only bilingual or culturally diverse needs to appropriately place those learners in special education as learning disabled or behaviorally disordered. Careful consideration of the behaviors exhibited by diverse learners relative to culture diversity and second language acquisition will facilitate the reduction of misdiagnosing a learning difference as a disability.

In addition, in order for appropriate diagnosis of a disability to occur, problem-solving teams must provide evidence of the identification of an intrinsic disorder reflecting cognitive and learning needs as discussed in this chapter. When considering all factors involved, educators will find that although behaviors and characteristics are similar, most diverse learners at-risk show evidence of needs related directly to cultural diversity and/or second language acquisition with no evidence of any intrinsic disorder. Chapter 4 will consider the assessment process used to identify whether the learning and behavior needs are most associated with diversity issues and/or disorders within the student.

SUMMARY

A variety of behaviors and learning characteristics reflecting cultural diversity and stages of second language acquisition were presented in this chapter. Also discussed were examples of practical definitions of learning disabilities and behavior disorders, including various behavioral characteristics often associated with these disabilities. Comparisons between diverse behaviors and disability behaviors were made along with discussions about the need to identify intrinsic disorders to appropriately identify a student as having a disability. The idea that most diverse learners exhibit behaviors in schools that reflect their cultural values and/or stages of second language acquisition, rather than intrinsic disorders, was also emphasized, highlighting the differentiation between learning differences and learning disorders.

Additional Activities to Support Learner Outcomes

1. Present to colleagues the behaviors typically associated with diverse cultural norms and values and compare these with expected school behaviors.

2. Develop a schoolwide plan and process to ensure that the diverse behaviors discussed in this chapter are not mistaken for behaviors indicating a disability.

3. Generate professional development suggestions to share with colleagues so that they acquire more expertise in differentiating learning differences from learning and behavior disorders.

4. Provide examples from your educational setting that support the reduction of misidentifying learning differences from disabilities.

Teacher _____ Date _____

Classroom Environment _____

Instructions: Using the scale, respond to each item as it relates to how you prefer to address teaching in your classroom environment. Any additional comments about your tendencies toward the style of Field may also be documented below.

1	2	3	4	5
Never		Sometimes		Always

To what extent do you:

1. Think in terms of parts and components of lessons   1 2 3 4 5

2. Emphasize the specific details of materials   1 2 3 4 5

3. Attempt to learn and internalize new ideas through the study of integrated components   1 2 3 4 5

4. Prefer to view ideas/tasks in a global way   1 2 3 4 5

5. Emphasize the gestalt, or whole, rather than isolated parts   1 2 3 4 5

6. React to a new task/lesson by first breaking it down into its subparts   1 2 3 4 5

7. Have difficulty separating the whole from its parts   1 2 3 4 5

8. Study ideas/topics as though they are comprised of many separate and distinct parts   1 2 3 4 5

9. Attempt to interrelate ideas in order to understand a topic   1 2 3 4 5

10. Prefer to analyze discrete elements, ideas, or topics   1 2 3 4 5

Scoring: Place the number marked for each item on the lines below and find the sum. Items marked with an asterisk (ᴬ) must be reversed scored (i.e., 1 = 5, 2 = 4, 4 = 2, 5 = 1).

Items: 1_____ 2_____ 3*_____ 4*_____ 5*_____ 6_____ 7*_____ 8_____ 9*_____ 10_____

Field Score: _____ divided by 10 = _____
         Sum   Score

Place an X on the continuum that corresponds with your score:

1	2	3	4	5
Dependent		Balanced		Independent

Summary Comments:

Student _____ Date _____

Classroom Environment _____ Teacher Completing Form _____

Instructions: Using the scale, respond to each item as it relates to how you observe the student learning in your classroom environment. Any additional comments about the learner's tendencies toward the style of Field may also be documented below.

1	2	3	4	5
Never		Sometimes		Always

To what extent does the student:

1.	Think in terms of parts and components of lessons	1	2	3	4	5
2.	Emphasize the specific details of materials	1	2	3	4	5
3.	Attempt to learn and internalize new ideas through the study of integrated components	1	2	3	4	5
4.	Prefer to view ideas/tasks in a global way	1	2	3	4	5
5.	Emphasize the gestalt, or whole, rather than isolated parts	1	2	3	4	5
6.	React to a new task/lesson by first breaking it down into its subparts	1	2	3	4	5
7.	Have difficulty separating the whole from its parts	1	2	3	4	5
8.	Study ideas/topics as though they are comprised of many separate and distinct parts	1	2	3	4	5
9.	Attempt to interrelate ideas in order to understand a topic	1	2	3	4	5
10.	Prefer to analyze discrete elements, ideas, or topics	1	2	3	4	5

Scoring: Place the number marked for each item on the lines below and find the sum. Items marked with an asterisk (*) must be reversed scored (i.e., 1 = 5; 2 = 4; 4 = 2; 5 = 1).

Items: 1____ 2____ 3*____ 4*____ 5*____ 6____ 7*____ 8____ 9*____ 10____

Field Score: _____ divided by 10 = _____
      Sum   Score

Place an X on the continuum that corresponds with your score:

_____

1	2	3	4	5
Dependent		Balanced		Independent

Summary Comments:

Teacher _____   Date _____

Classroom Environment _____

Instructions: Using the scale, respond to each item as it relates to how you prefer to address teaching in your classroom environment. Any additional comments about your tendencies toward the style of Tempo may also be documented below.

1	2	3	4	5
Never		Sometimes		Always

To what extent do you:

1. Take extra care in what you do in the classroom   1 2 3 4 5

2. Move from one lesson to another quickly   1 2 3 4 5

3. Approach tasks in the classroom one step at a time   1 2 3 4 5

4. Pursue any avenue that makes sense at the time   1 2 3 4 5

5. Regularly review lessons/material to improve classroom performance   1 2 3 4 5

6. Prefer to have more than one lesson/activity occurring at the same time   1 2 3 4 5

7. Prefer to have lessons build on each other in a sequence   1 2 3 4 5

8. Follow any path available to make a point   1 2 3 4 5

9. Take time to bridge one lesson/activity to another   1 2 3 4 5

10. Respond to tasks/activities in a quick manner   1 2 3 4 5

Scoring: Place the number marked for each item on the lines below and find the sum. Items marked with an asterisk (*) must be reversed scored (i.e., 1 = 5; 2 = 4; 4 = 2; 5 = 1).

Items: 1____   2*____   3____   4*____   5____   6*____   7____   8*____   9____   10*____

Tempo Score: _____ divided by 10 = _____
                          Sum   Score

Place an X on the continuum that corresponds with your score:

_____

1	2	3	4	5
Impulsive		Balanced		Reflective

Summary Comments:

Student _____ Date _____

Classroom Environment _____ Teacher Completing Form _____

Instructions: Using the scale, respond to each item as it relates to how you observe the student learning in your classroom environment. Any additional comments about the learner's tendencies toward the style of Tempo may also be documented below.

1	2	3	4	5
Never		Sometimes		Always

To what extent does the student:

1. Take extra care in what he or she does in the classroom   1   2   3   4   5

2. Move from one lesson to another quickly   1   2   3   4   5

3. Approach tasks in the classroom one step at a time   1   2   3   4   5

4. Pursue any avenue that makes sense at the time   1   2   3   4   5

5. Regularly review lessons/material to improve classroom performance   1   2   3   4   5

6. Prefer to have more than one lesson/activity occurring at the same time   1   2   3   4   5

7. Prefer to have lessons build on each other in a sequence   1   2   3   4   5

8. Follow any path available to make a point   1   2   3   4   5

9. Take time to bridge one lesson/activity to another   1   2   3   4   5

10. Respond to tasks/activities in a quick manner   1   2   3   4   5

Scoring: Place the number marked for each item on the lines below and find the sum. Items marked with an asterisk (*) must be reversed scored (i.e., 1 = 5; 2 = 4; 4 = 2; 5 = 1).

Items: 1____ 2*____ 3____ 4*____ 5____ 6*____ 7____ 8*____ 9____ 10*____

Tempo Score: _____ divided by 10 = _____
             Sum   Score

Place an X on the continuum that corresponds with your score:

_____

1	2	3	4	5
Impulsive		Balanced		Reflective

Summary Comments:

FORM 3.5 Teacher Self-Evaluation Instructional Style Guide: Tolerance

Teacher _____ Date _____

Classroom Environment _____

Instructions: Using the scale, respond to each item as it relates to how you prefer to address teaching in your classroom environment. Any additional comments about your tendencies toward the style of Tolerance may also be documented below.

1	2	3	4	5
Never		Sometimes		Always

To what extent do you:

1. Use fantasy in most lessons or ideas   1 2 3 4 5

2. Prefer clarity and structure   1 2 3 4 5

3. Meet expectations by following established rules   1 2 3 4 5

4. Make changes to meet needs in the classroom   1 2 3 4 5

5. Present material/work in own individual style   1 2 3 4 5

6. Take things as they are with little resistance   1 2 3 4 5

7. Complete tasks the correct way irregardless of support   1 2 3 4 5

8. Use imaginative approaches in the classroom   1 2 3 4 5

9. Take charge with little or no structure   1 2 3 4 5

10. Focus on making activities/assignments down to earth   1 2 3 4 5

Scoring: Place the number marked for each item on the lines below and find the sum. Items marked with an asterisk (*) must be reversed scored (i.e., 1 = 5; 2 = 4; 4 = 2; 5 = 1).

Items: 1____   2*____   3*____   4____   5____   6*____   7*____   8____   9____   10*____

Tolerance Score: _____ divided by 10 = _____
                   Sum   Score

Place an X on the continuum that corresponds with your score:

_____

1	2	3	4	5
Low		Balanced		High

Summary Comments:

FORM 3.6   Student Evaluation Instructional Style Guide: Tolerance

Student _____   Date _____

Classroom Environment _____   Teacher Completing Form _____

Instructions: Using the scale, respond to each item as it relates to how you observe the student most prefers to address learning in your classroom environment. Any additional comments about the learner's tendencies toward the style of Tolerance may also be documented below.

1	2	3	4	5
Never		Sometimes		Always

To what extent does the student:

1. Use fantasy in most lessons or ideas	1 2 3 4 5
2. Prefer clarity and structure	1 2 3 4 5
3. Meet expectations by following established rules	1 2 3 4 5
4. Make changes to meet needs in the classroom	1 2 3 4 5
5. Present material/work in own individual style	1 2 3 4 5
6. Take things as they are with little resistance	1 2 3 4 5
7. Complete tasks the correct way irregardless of support	1 2 3 4 5
8. Use imaginative approaches in the classroom	1 2 3 4 5
9. Take charge with little or no structure	1 2 3 4 5
10. Focus on making activities/assignments down to earth	1 2 3 4 5

Scoring: Place the number marked for each item on the lines below and find the sum.
Items marked with an asterisk (*) must be reversed scored (i.e., 1 = 5; 2 = 4; 4 = 2; 5 = 1).

Items: 1____   2*____   3*____   4____   5____   6*____   7*____   8____   9____   10*____

Tolerance Score: _____ divided by 10 = _____
                        Sum   Score

Place an X on the continuum that corresponds with your score:

_____

1	2	3	4	5
Low		Balanced		High

Summary Comments:

FORM 3.7 Teacher Self-Evaluation Instructional Style Guide: Categorization

Teacher _____ Date _____

Classroom Environment _____

Instructions: Using the scale, respond to each item as it relates to how you prefer to address teaching in your classroom environment. Any additional comments about your tendencies toward the style of Categorization may also be documented below.

1	2	3	4	5
Never		Sometimes		Always

To what extent do you:

1. Include as many primary and secondary ideas as possible when discussing a topic   1 2 3 4 5

2. Pay specific attention to the smallest details   1 2 3 4 5

3. Prefer to use general categories when grouping items to ensure that nothing is omitted   1 2 3 4 5

4. Include only selective details when presenting a topic   1 2 3 4 5

5. Exclude doubtful items or ideas when categorizing   1 2 3 4 5

6. Prefer to initially include many items in a grouping and then discard the unnecessary ones   1 2 3 4 5

7. Split topics apart into their distinct elements   1 2 3 4 5

8. Summarize all points of an activity or lesson   1 2 3 4 5

9. Cluster items together only when they possess identical characteristics   1 2 3 4 5

10. Use outlines to identify all or most elements/ideas when completing tasks   1 2 3 4 5

Scoring: Place the number marked for each item on the lines below and find the sum. Items marked with an asterisk (*) must be reversed scored (i.e., 1 = 5; 2 = 4; 4 = 2; 5 = 1).

Items: 1____ 2*____ 3____ 4*____ 5*____ 6____ 7*____ 8____ 9*____ 10____

Categorization Score: _____ divided by 10 = _____
                 Sum   Score

Place an X on the continuum that corresponds with your score:

1	2	3	4	5
Narrow		Balanced		Broad

Summary Comments:

Student Evaluation Instructional Style Guide: Categorization

Student _____ Date _____

Classroom Environment _____ Teacher Completing Form _____

Instructions: Using the scale, respond to each item as it relates to how you observe the student learning in your classroom environment. Any additional comments about the learner's tendencies toward the style of Categorization may also be documented below.

1	2	3	4	5
Never		Sometimes		Always

To what extent does the student:

1. Include as many primary and secondary ideas as possible when discussing a topic   1   2   3   4   5

2. Pay specific attention to the smallest details   1   2   3   4   5

3. Prefer to use general categories when grouping items to ensure that nothing is omitted   1   2   3   4   5

4. Include only selective details when presenting a topic   1   2   3   4   5

5. Exclude doubtful items or ideas when categorizing   1   2   3   4   5

6. Prefer to initially include many items in a grouping and then discard the unnecessary ones   1   2   3   4   5

7. Split topics apart into their distinct elements   1   2   3   4   5

8. Summarize all points of an activity or lesson   1   2   3   4   5

9. Cluster items together only when they possess identical characteristics   1   2   3   4   5

10. Use outlines to identify all or most elements/ideas when completing tasks   1   2   3   4   5

Scoring: Place the number marked for each item on the lines below and find the sum. Items marked with an asterisk (*) must be reversed scored (i.e., 1 = 5; 2 = 4; 4 = 2; 5 = 1).

Items: 1____   2*____   3____   4*____   5*____   6____   7*____   8____   9*____   10____

Categorization Score: _____ divided by 10 = _____

                       Sum   Score

Place an X on the continuum that corresponds with your score:

_____

1	2	3	4	5
Narrow		Balanced		Broad

Summary Comments:

Teacher _____   Date _____

Classroom Environment _____

Instructions: Using the scale, respond to each item as it relates to how you prefer to address teaching in your classroom environment. Any additional comments about your tendencies toward the style of Persistence may also be documented below.

1	2	3	4	5
Never		Sometimes		Always

To what extent do you:

1.	Avoid making changes unless absolutely necessary	1 2 3 4 5
2.	Consider yourself highly structured in the way classroom situations are approached	1 2 3 4 5
3.	Rely heavily on scanning and skimming abilities	1 2 3 4 5
4.	Prefer to use several short blocks of time rather than one longer segment of time to complete a task	1 2 3 4 5
5.	Avoid tasks that are highly structured	1 2 3 4 5
6.	Take extended periods of time to carefully review new material or implement activities	1 2 3 4 5
7.	Welcome the chance to undertake tasks that require extended periods of time to complete	1 2 3 4 5
8.	Work on tasks until they are completed no matter how long it takes	1 2 3 4 5
9.	Experience difficulty working on tasks or activities for extended periods of time	1 2 3 4 5
10.	Tend to be unstructured in completing classroom activities or lessons	1 2 3 4 5

Scoring: Place the number marked for each item on the lines below and find the sum. Items marked with an asterisk (*) must be reversed scored (i.e., 1 = 5; 2 = 4; 4 = 2; 5 = 1).

Items: 1_____   2_____   3*_____   4*_____   5*_____   6_____   7_____   8_____   9*_____   10*_____

Persistence Score: _____ divided by 10 = _____
                          Sum   Score

Place an X on the continuum that corresponds with your score:

_____

1	2	3	4	5
Low		Balanced		High

Summary Comments:

Student _____ Date _____

Classroom Environment _____ Teacher Completing Form _____

Instructions: Using the scale, respond to each item as it relates to how you observe the student learning in your classroom environment. Any additional comments about the learner's tendencies toward the style of Persistence may also be documented below.

1	2	3	4	5
Never		Sometimes		Always

To what extent does the student:

1. Avoid making changes unless absolutely necessary   1 2 3 4 5

2. Consider himself or herself highly structured in the way classroom situations are approached   1 2 3 4 5

3. Rely heavily on scanning and skimming abilities   1 2 3 4 5

4. Prefer to use several short blocks of time rather than one longer segment of time to complete a task   1 2 3 4 5

5. Avoid tasks that are highly structured   1 2 3 4 5

6. Take extended periods of time to carefully review new material or implement activities   1 2 3 4 5

7. Welcome the chance to undertake tasks that require extended periods of time to complete   1 2 3 4 5

8. Work on tasks until they are completed no matter how long it takes   1 2 3 4 5

9. Experience difficulty working on tasks or activities for extended periods of time   1 2 3 4 5

10. Tend to be unstructured in completing classroom activities or lessons   1 2 3 4 5

Scoring: Place the number marked for each item on the lines below and find the sum. Items marked with an asterisk (*) must be reversed scored (i.e., 1 = 5; 2 = 4; 4 = 2; 5 = 1).

Items: 1____ 2____ 3*____ 4*____ 5*____ 6____ 7____ 8____ 9*____ 10*____

Persistence Score: _____ divided by 10 = _____
                 Sum   Score

Place an X on the continuum that corresponds with your score:

1	2	3	4	5
Low		Balanced		High

Summary Comments:

Teacher _____ Student _____ Date _____

Instructions: Information obtained from completion of the Teacher Self-Evaluation Guides and Student Evaluation Guides is summarized on this form. Place an X along the continuum reflecting the obtained score from completion of the associated guides.

▶ **Field**

Teacher	1	2	3	4	5
	Dependent		Balanced		Independent

Student	1	2	3	4	5
	Dependent		Balanced		Independent

▶ **Tempo**

Teacher	1	2	3	4	5
	Impulsive		Balanced		Reflective

Student	1	2	3	4	5
	Impulsive		Balanced		Reflective

▶ **Tolerance**

Teacher	1	2	3	4	5
	Low		Balanced		High

Student	1	2	3	4	5
	Low		Balanced		High

▶ **Categorization**

Teacher	1	2	3	4	5
	Narrow		Balanced		Broad

Student	1	2	3	4	5
	Narrow		Balanced		Broad

▶ **Persistence**

Teacher	1	2	3	4	5
	Low		Balanced		High

Student	1	2	3	4	5
	Low		Balanced		High

Teacher _____ Student _____ Date _____

Area of Need or Suspected Problem _____

Instructions: Rate each item relative to its instructional consideration by the problem-solving team to clarify the learner's educational needs within a cultural and linguistic framework. Provide clarifying comments as a summary of the ratings.

  1 = No Consideration   3 = Considered to Some Extent

  2 = Very Little Consideration   4 = Extensively Considered

The extent to which the following are considered in the decision-making process:

Second Language Acquisition

Learner's attitude/motivation	1	2	3	4
Native language proficiency	1	2	3	4
Role of family/community	1	2	3	4
Compatibility between teaching and learning styles	1	2	3	4
Learner's stage of second language acquisition	1	2	3	4
Interlangauge (utilization of internal language system)	1	2	3	4
Code-switching abilities and usage	1	2	3	4
Linguistic features relative to comprehension	1	2	3	4

Cultural Diversity

Acculturation process and associated stress levels	1	2	3	4
Preference toward cooperative vs. competitive learning	1	2	3	4
Presence of active rather than passive learning	1	2	3	4
Assertive or aggressive behaviors as cultural values	1	2	3	4
Locus of control	1	2	3	4
Instructional styles of learner (Persistence, Tolerance, etc.)	1	2	3	4
Significance of nonverbal communications in learning	1	2	3	4
Varied perceptions of concepts of time and space	1	2	3	4

Disability Characteristics

Attention deficits	1	2	3	4
Impulsivity	1	2	3	4
Hyperactivity	1	2	3	4
Information-processing deficits	1	2	3	4
Extreme emotional response to learning	1	2	3	4
Responsiveness to interventions	1	2	3	4

Summary of discussions about cultural and linguistic influences on learner's suspected area of educational need:

CHAPTER 4

Culturally Responsive Assessment

▶ Significance to Contemporary Educational Contexts

IF MULTI-TIERED RESPONSE TO INTERVENTION is to be successful with culturally and linguistically diverse learners it must assist educators to more effectively reduce bias in the assessment process and associated uses of assessment devices. Ultimately, the proper selection and use of appropriate assessment devices with diverse learners determines the extent to which educators accurately interpret assessment results. This is significant in today's schools since the more accurate the progress monitoring, the less likely the misdiagnosing of learning differences as disabilities will occur. Culturally responsive education provides diverse learners the best opportunity to receive unbiased instruction through multi-tiered interventions, along with associated response to intervention progress monitoring and assessment.

▶ Overview

This chapter discusses specific features to ensure that the assessment of diverse learners is culturally valid relative to the interactions among language, culture, and disability needs addressed in the previous chapter. The topics addressed in this chapter focus on consideration of the selection of appropriate assessment devices and use of assessment processes that reflect cultural and linguistic needs, while avoiding misinterpreting learning differences as a disability for diverse students.

▶ Key Topics

- ▶ current diversity assessment issues
- ▶ assessment bias
- ▶ assessment gap
- ▶ culturally valid assessment
- ▶ assessment competence
- ▶ cultural and linguistic factors in assessment
- ▶ application of diverse qualities in RTI

▶ Learner Outcomes

Upon completion of this chapter, the reader will be able to:

1. Articulate components to conduct a culturally valid assessment.
2. Reduce bias in assessment practices.
3. Specify cultural and linguistic considerations to several important assessment variables in understanding and implementing effective assessment.
4. Discuss the assessment implications of addressing six major cultural and linguistic factors when assessing diverse learners.
5. Articulate and implement culturally valid assessment to properly diagnose a learning difference from a disability.

For over a century, educators have subjected children and adults to an enormous amount of testing to identify problems, disabilities, strengths, weaknesses, interests, skills, knowledge, intelligence, and aptitude. Over the years, we have used assessments for screening, diagnosing, placing, removing, returning, or otherwise classifying learners. Today, within the parameters of multi-tiered instruction, we use assessment to monitor progress and determine response to interventions (RTI). These discussions focus specifically on cultural/linguistic issues; for more comprehensive coverage of assessment in today's schools the reader is referred to McMillan (2001), Salvia and Ysseldyke (2003), and Yates and Ortiz (2004). For our purposes, I have selected several of the primary components within a comprehensive assessment from which misinterpretation of learning differences as disabilities tends to occur. These are identified along with practical suggestions and guides for establishing a more culturally responsive assessment process for diverse learners. This chapter discusses several factors and elements important to an effective assessment process, providing examples of ways to employ them in culturally responsive ways, while Chapter 5 discusses various assessment practices used to determine learning differences from disabilities.

Achievement Gap and Diverse Learners

One of the most fundamental questions challenging educators in today's schools is, "How can we reduce the achievement gap experienced by diverse learners?" The contents of this book are designed, in part, to assist in appropriately responding to this question. A brief overview of existing achievement gaps is warranted to make certain that all educators are aware of this problem and its relationship to differentiating learning differences from learning and behavior disorders. Clearly, a greater understanding of learning differences from disabilities in diverse learners will assist in reducing achievement gaps due to more appropriate education.

The *achievement gap* refers to a disparity in academic achievement between groups of students. According to the U.S. Department of Education (2003a, b), 39 percent of white students demonstrated proficiency or higher in fourth grade reading compared to only 12 percent and 14 percent of African American and Hispanic students, respectively. In fourth grade math, 42 percent of white students were proficient or higher compared to 10 percent and 15 percent of African American and Hispanic students, respectively. This represents an achievement gap of over 25 percent in reading and 27 percent in math for these diverse learners. Explanations of contributing factors causing these achievement gaps are many, including poverty, quality of teaching, environmental factors, or health

Selecting Assessment Instruments

Cultural and linguistic bias in testing instruments continues to facilitate the misinterpretation of learning differences as disabilities. When using standardized assessment devices with diverse learners, several issues must be addressed to ensure that results accurately reflect knowledge and skills, rather than reflecting cultural or language biases. Form 4.1 provides a checklist for educators so that they can ensure that nonbias, culturally valid testing occurs. The items on this form were initially developed from information found in Figueroa and Newsome (2004), Wilkinson, Ortiz, and Robertson-Courtney (2004), Lachat (2004), and O'Malley and Pierce (1996), as found in Hoover et al. (2008).

▶ **Cultural Assessment Significance:** When considering the tests utilized with diverse learners, problem-solving teams must be confident that the results are accurate for the educational areas assessed. The confidence level should be documented by the problem-solving team, providing evidence that clearly illustrates that the testing instrument is unbiased and appropriate for use with diverse learners. Simply using an assessment device because it exists or is used with everyone else is not sufficient when cultural and/or linguistic diversity exists. An analysis of the testing device using Form 4.1 will assist in determining level of confidence in using that instrument with the diverse learner in question. Lack of confidence in the instrument, based on an objective evaluation using items in Form 4.1, is a "red flag" alerting the problem-solving teams to the potential limited usefulness and relevance of the results.

Culturally Valid Assessment Competence

Cultural competence relative to testing requires an understanding of at least two aspects that potentially relate to biased assessment (Hoover et al., 2008). These are:

1. *Reliability/Validity.* An instrument's validity and reliability serve as the foundation for making informed decisions concerning selection and use of the device. *Validity* refers to the extent to which the test measures what it says it is measuring; *reliability* refers to the extent to which the test scores are consistent over time (McMillan, 2001). An instrument may have reliability without being valid; however, a valid instrument is also reliable. An example of a reliable instrument that lacks validity occurs when a test yields consistent scores but does not accurately measure what it purports to measure (i.e., the test provides a consistent reading grade level but the test's ability to assess reading is questionable or invalid). Validity is of primary concern to problem-solving teams since many tests do not reflect a sufficient representation of the diverse population in

the norming and standardization procedures. Problem-solving teams need to know and understand the validity and reliability of a selected device relative to the diverse population in question.

▶ **Cultural Assessment Significance:** Use of an instrument that lacks sufficient validity and reliability for use with the diverse population in question perpetuates the misdiagnosis of learning differences as disabilities. Problem-solving teams need to be accountable for clearly showing how the selected instrument is valid and reliable for the struggling learner based on the testing development procedures, sampling, and geographic distribution as discussed in the test's technical manual.

2. *Construction of Standardized Instruments.* The manner in which standardized tests are structured may also create issues for diverse learners. For example, some standardized tests are constructed and normed so that the difficulty of items increases from the beginning to the end of the test. Therefore, a progression of item difficulty becomes a potential bias for some diverse learners because they may need more time to progress through the test. As previously emphasized, if diverse learners are simply provided additional time to complete the test, their true knowledge and skills may be more accurately assessed. However, due to the standardization procedures, additional time is often not granted. Therefore, these tests may not be appropriate for use with diverse students as they will not accurately determine what the student knows due to insufficient time to complete test items resulting from various cultural or linguistic factors.

▶ **Cultural Assessment Significance:** Assuming the device is valid and reliable, if diverse learners are provided additional time to complete standardized instruments they may more accurately assess student knowledge and skills. This, in turn, enables the problem-solving team to discern a learning difference from a disability. Problem-solving teams should address the following question prior to accepting standardized test results: *If the student was provided additional time needed, due to cultural or linguistic difference, will more accurate results be generated?*

Cultural and Linguistic Assessment Factors

Culturally responsive assessment is grounded in efforts to ensure that the learner's cultural and linguistic diversity are considered integral to the overall decision-making process. When considering specific classroom practices in education, Tharp (1997) and the Center for Research on Education, Diversity and

Excellence (CREDE) identified five standards designed to reflect culturally responsive education.

Standard	Description
1. Linguistic Competence	Appropriate instruction; functional language usage; purposeful conversations; connection between current and prior experiences
2. Contextualized Learning	Home/community culture and student experiences are reflected in instruction
3. Joint Productivity	Activities shared by teachers/students; interactive conversations
4. Instructional Conversation	On-going teacher–student dialogue; form, exchange, and express ideas interactively
5. Challenging Curriculum	Curriculum must be appropriate and effective in challenging students cognitively

These standards provide a foundation to effective instruction for culturally and linguistically diverse learners. They also provide structure to identifying specific factors that reflect various diverse needs in the classroom. Hoover et al. (2008), Hoover and Patton (2004), and Hoover (2001) discuss six cultural and linguistic factors associated with the CREDE standards that are essential to the culturally responsive assessment process as discussed in different sources (Baca, 2005; Banks, 1994; Lachat, 2004; Rueda & Kim, 2001; Tharp, 1997). Table 4.1 summarizes these factors.

Each of these six factors has already been introduced and discussed in the previous chapter. They are summarized here along with specific reference to decision-making implications to discern learning differences from disabilities. Overall, these six cultural/linguistic factors must be assessed and understood by problem-solving teams to provide a culturally responsive assessment process for diverse learners. Lack of knowledge in any of these six areas significantly reduces the problem-solving team's ability to accurately make informed decisions.

Acculturation

Adapting to a new cultural environment, which for some learners is highly stressful, often results in behaviors such as withdrawal, confusion with locus of control, or anxiety (Baca & Cervantes, 2004). The frequency of these expected behaviors is reduced as the learner becomes more acculturated, and educators need to avoid misinterpreting these behaviors as disorders requiring special education.

▶ **Difference/Disability Implications:** Problem-solving teams must consider the learner's behaviors within an acculturative context. If the behaviors are associated with acculturation they should be expected and in most situations will diminish over time. Therefore, problem-solving teams must consider time and opportunity associated with acculturation, and if either of these is limited, the greater the impact acculturative stress may have on the learner. The team's sensitivity to acculturation needs and behaviors will avoid misdiagnosing these behaviors as a disorder. Form 4.2, Guide to Identify Acculturation Needs, provides

TABLE 4.1 Cultural/Linguistic Factors in Determining Difference from Disability

Cultural/Linguistic Factor	Significance to Decision-Making	Key Points to Consider
Language Functions (Conversational/Academic)	Student's conversational language is important to build a foundation to learning; academic language is critical to succeed with more conceptually challenging academic tasks	Verbal interactions are critical to the development of a second language; both fluency and accuracy must be identified; ability to interpret and convey meaning is also essential for academic success
Acculturation	Students from varied cultural and linguistic backgrounds often face tremendous challenges adapting to new cultural environments and unfamiliar school-based academic and behavioral expectations	Acculturation (i.e., adapting to a new cultural environment) often leads to stress, withdrawal, or various levels of acting-out behaviors. These are expected behaviors, not disordered behaviors, and will subside as the learner becomes more acculturated and familiar with academic and social expectations in school
Conceptual Knowledge/ Experiential Background	The foundation to acquiring new knowledge and skills is found in a student's existing abilities based on prior academic, social, and life experiences	Understanding a learner's prior and current conceptual knowledge and prior experiential background helps educators to understand a learner's abilities to deal with hierarchies and connections among curricular concepts, knowledge, and skills
Higher-Order Thinking Abilities	In order to best determine students' true abilities, they must be taught within a cognitively challenging curriculum where opportunities to use higher-level thinking abilities are provided	Knowledge of student use of higher-order thinking abilities helps educators understand how the student interacts with and learns curricular content, knowledge, and skills
Cultural Values/Norms	Diverse learners bring a variety of cultural customs and values as well as languages to their educational environments	Meaningful classroom instruction must be culturally responsive to best educate diverse learners and interpret academic progress
Teaching/Learning Styles	Students from diverse cultures may possess various learning style preferences reflective of cultural norms and teachings that may differ from teaching styles found in U.S. classrooms	Diverse learners may use different reasoning strategies reflective of their own cultural values and/or second language acquisition stage; these may result in a mismatch between preferred styles of learning and classroom teaching styles— a mismatch that should not be misinterpreted as a disability

process of acquiring English need to be taught " in ways that will enable them to respond to the more complex and cognitively demanding tasks" (p. 104). While diverse learners acquiring a second language may experience temporary problems using higher-order thinking abilities in English, they may be quite skilled at comprehension, synthesis, evaluation, or analysis in their first language.

▶ **Difference/Disability Implications:** Problem-solving teams must include discussion of student use of higher-level thinking in the first language (e.g., Russian, Vietnamese, Spanish) if he or she is in the process of acquiring English as a second language. Inability to adequately employ higher-order thinking abilities in English when use of these skills does not pose problems in the native language is an indication that a learning disorder does not exist. Teams must document student use of higher-level thinking abilities along with evidence that the curriculum facilitates use of higher-order thinking before making any determination that a learning disability exists.

SUMMARY

Culturally responsive assessment requires that the learner's cultural and linguistic experiences are considered. These factors are especially important to the process as students are considered for Tier 2 or 3 instruction. Simply relying on data scores without considering various cultural and linguistic factors with diverse learners perpetuates the lack of culturally responsive assessment, thereby leading to erroneous decisions and misdiagnosis of learning problems. In order for RTI to be effective for all learners it must lead to a reduction of inappropriate referrals to special education, and further clarify learning differences from suspected disabilities by implementing culturally responsive assessment.

▶ ## Additional Activities to Support Learner Outcomes

1. Determine your school's policies concerning assessment of culturally and linguistically diverse learners.

2. Evaluate extent to which the six cultural and linguistic factors (i.e., acculturation, experiential background, etc.) discussed in this chapter are addressed in the assessment of diverse learners.

3. Identify one assessment issue (e.g., timed tests, bias in assessment) for diverse learners presented in the chapter and investigate how your school/district addresses the issue.

4. Develop and implement a presentation on the importance of factors associated with a test's validity when used with diverse learners.

FORM 4.1 Determining Cultural Responsiveness and Validity of
Assessment Device for Use with Diverse Learners

Student _____

Assessment Device _____

Check each item as it applies to the assessment device. Provide comments to clarify item for learner.
Attach this completed guide to the device's protocol after administration.

_____ Device contains culturally valid, appropriate/responsive topics, content, and examples.
Comments:

_____ Device has been researched, developed, and validated to include use with diverse learners.
Comments:

_____ Test manual describes steps undertaken to include cultural and linguistic diversity in the development, standardization, and norming of the device.
Comments:

_____ If device is a translated test, manual describes proper translation procedures completed by culturally responsive test development personnel.
Comments:

_____ The student tested possesses experiential background sufficient to be familiar with the concepts and vocabulary on the device.
Comments:

_____ Second language acquisition needs are accounted for in the time restrictions associated with completing the assessment device.
Comments:

_____ Students acquiring English as a second language are provided sufficient opportunities (similar to English speakers) to demonstrate knowledge and skills assessed by the device.
Comments:

_____ Learner is familiar with the format of the device (e.g., short answer, multiple choice, true/false).
Comments:

_____ The testing manual describes appropriate uses and/or limitations in the use of the device with diverse learners.
Comments:

_____ The language of the device is in the student's most proficient language, which for some may be a language other than English.
Comments:

_____ If test is in English, learner possesses sufficient English language skills necessary to complete the assessment device.
Comments:

FORM 4.2 Guide to Understanding Acculturation Needs

Student _____

Educator Completing Guide _____ Date _____

Instructions: Respond to each factor based on information gathered from interviews, review of records, and/or observations.

Student's gender: _____

Student's first culture: _____

Student's native language: _____

Student's English language proficiency level: ____ Non   ____ Limited   ____ Proficient

Age at time of family's arrival in the U.S.: _____   ____ Born in U.S.

Current grade level: _____

Entrance status to U.S.:   ____ Immigrant   ____ Refugee

Number of generations family has been residing in the U.S.:   ____ 1   ____ 2   ____ 3 or more

Number of months child has been exposed to the European/American culture: _____

What is the learner's:

Previous experience with other cultures?

Involvement with people from other cultures?

Compatibility between native and second culture?

Attitude toward the second culture?

Relationship with members of the first and second culture?

Level of native language support within first culture?

Level of cultural values support within first culture?

Diversity within home community?

Preference to maintain first culture/language?

CHAPTER 5

Selecting and Using Culturally Responsive Assessment Practices

▶ Significance to Contemporary Educational Contexts

Within the overall context of a culturally responsive assessment process and use of formal and informal assessment devices is the selection and use of a variety of assessment practices. As discussed, student progress is monitored on a regular and consistent basis as part of multi-tiered instruction (i.e., response to intervention). Problem-solving teams have several different assessment practices available to them, and if implemented in culturally responsive ways, will assist teams to more clearly understand learning differences from disabilities. This is of particular significance for diverse learners in today's classrooms since the implementation of multi-tiered or multi-layered instruction utilizing evidence-based interventions purports to more adequately meet a variety of educational and social-emotional needs. The selection and use of various assessment practices is integral to implementing multi-tiered learning and measuring, in culturally responsive ways, learner response to the interventions. The wide range of diverse linguistic and cultural backgrounds that students bring to today's classrooms necessitates the strategic use of a variety of assessment practices implemented within a culturally responsive assessment process discussed in the previous chapter.

▶ Overview

Based on the assessment foundation discussed in the previous chapter, Chapter 5 discusses several assessment practices that are appropriate for use with culturally and linguistically diverse learners. The practices presented in this chapter complement standardized assessment as well as serve to support on-going progress-monitoring efforts to measure response to intervention. Specific applications for use with diverse learners of each assessment practice are provided along with selected guides to assist problem-solving teams to differentiate learning differences from disabilities. The use of assessment accommodations with diverse learners follows the presentation of the twelve selected assessment practices.

▶ Key Topics

- ▶ analytic teaching
- ▶ interviews, observations, and review of records
- ▶ language samples
- ▶ work sample analysis
- ▶ task analysis
- ▶ curriculum-based measurement
- ▶ performance-based assessment
- ▶ running records
- ▶ portfolio assessment
- ▶ functional behavioral assessment
- ▶ assessment accommodations

▶ Learner Outcomes

Upon completion of this chapter, the reader will be able to:

1. Apply various assessment practices in culturally responsive ways.
2. Describe the steps necessary to implement culturally responsive assessment practices.
3. Use authentic assessment practices in progress monitoring of diverse learners' response to instruction.
4. Identify specific assessment accommodations appropriate for use with diverse learners.
5. Describe various assessment practices to others showing how they assist in reducing misinterpretation of learning differences as disabilities.

INTRODUCTION

A variety of assessment practices exist that complement the use of standardized devices to determine learner abilities. Several different assessment practices, supported by research, are presented in Table 5.1. As will be discussed, when used within the overall context of a culturally valid assessment process, these practices will provide problem-solving teams valuable and meaningful information about diverse learners. The selected evidence-based practices are not all-inclusive; however, they represent those that reduce misinterpretation of learning differences as disorders due to the flexibility inherent within each to focus on diverse issues.

In addition, similar to the testing instruments, misuse of the various assessment practices that follow may perpetuate misinterpretation of learning differences as disabilities. Form 5.1, Guide to Non-Discriminatory Implementation of Assessment Practices, provides a checklist so that implementation of these assessment practices will best meet diverse learners' needs. The guide, derived from discussions in Hoover et al. (2008) and Baca and Cervantes (2004), helps to clarify the implementation of these twelve assessment practices in culturally responsive and nonbiased ways.

As shown in Table 5.1 (developed from information found in Hoover et al. [2008] and Hoover [2001]), assessment must reflect learners' diverse needs associated with culture and second language development. Adherence to these items will facilitate the culturally responsive implementation of assessment practices for diverse learners, with the ultimate outcome being reduction in misinterpreting cultural and linguistic diversity as learning or behavioral disabilities. In addition, minimizing the problems previously discussed when using standardized testing with diverse learners is best accomplished through the use of a variety of authentic assessment practices. Use of authentic practices enables educators to observe, record, and present learner needs and accomplishments in culturally valid ways. The twelve selected assessment practices follow, including use with diverse learners.

Analytic Teaching

Overview

Analytic teaching is an evidence-based intervention, which may also be referred to as *diagnostic* or *prescriptive teaching*. Educators observe learner behaviors within structured educational tasks, including subdividing tasks if necessary, in order to gain increased knowledge about student performance and needs (Moran & Malott, 2004).

■ *Relevant Uses.* Analytic teaching is effective for implementing systematic adaptations to instruction and monitoring student progress relative to those adaptations (de Valenzuela & Baca, 2004). It provides insight into how learners

TABLE 5.1 Assessment Practices

Assessment Practice	Purpose in Assessment	Cultural Responsiveness
Analytic Teaching	Analyze learner behaviors while engaged in specific task designed to target identified behaviors	As student engages in tasks, diverse needs may be observed, documented, and considered in the analysis of observed student behaviors
Cross-Cultural Interview	Discuss cultural and linguistic background of learner and determine if behaviors are reflective of cultural and linguistic background	Provides parents and significant others in the student's life opportunity to share cultural values, norms, and teaching
Language Samples	Obtain documented samples of student uses of language, both L1 and L2, to analyze thinking skills, vocabulary, and contextual uses	Language samples reflect second language acquisition behaviors, which can be put into a proper cultural context to assess differences from disabilities
Classroom Observations	Obtain firsthand knowledge of student academic and socioemotional behaviors exhibited in the instructional environment	Appropriate cultural and linguistic opportunities to learn can be determined and evaluated through periodic observations
Review Existing Records	Put learner characteristics into a historical context, determine prior interventions used, and ascertain perceptions of previous teachers	Records allow educators to gain a greater understanding of the learner's cultural and linguistic background and experiences
Work Samples Analysis	Identify patterns, consistencies, and strengths in student work	Diverse linguistic needs of second language learners and those experiencing acculturation may become more apparent through analysis of work samples
Task Analysis	Assist in analyzing student strengths and weaknesses through the breakdown of tasks into discrete parts and subtasks	Cultural and linguistic preferences and needs can be incorporated into task analysis to better assess second language behaviors and associated cultural teachings
Curriculum-Based Measurement	Evidence-based strategy for measuring student progress in a systematic way using valid measures	Systematic method using valid measures generates nonbiased classroom performance progress monitoring for diverse learners
Performance-Based Assessment	Assessment practice where student progress is monitored through evaluation of a constructed response or product	Assessment practice that allows diverse learners opportunities to demonstrate skill proficiency in culturally/linguistically responsive ways
Running Records	Record over defined period of time reading behaviors of beginning readers while reading for a specified amount of time (e.g., ten minutes)	Cultural and linguistic needs may be more accurately observed through running records as well as learner response to reading interventions
Portfolio Assessment	Assessment process during which students compile a collection of work designed to illustrate their educational knowledge, skills, and growth	Authentic method for evaluating student progress while simultaneously allowing diverse learners to demonstrate growth consistent with cultural/linguistic values and norms
Functional Behavioral Assessment (FBA)	A technique based on the premise that behavior serves some meaningful function for the learner	Since FBA considers environmental conditions relative to the behaviors, this may include cultural and linguistic values/norms

engage in tasks as well as the process they follow to complete the tasks. As an assessment practice, by documenting what the student is capable of and/or struggling to complete, additional information about diverse learners' needs are recorded. Hammill (1987) wrote that analytic teaching provides useful information to: (1) form hypotheses concerning the needs of students; (2) identify necessary subsequent steps in assessment or instruction; and (3) progress monitor learner responses to the intervention implemented.

■ *Steps/Process.* The following steps are undertaken to implement analytic teaching:

1. Identify current instructional condition or baseline performance.
2. Select an instructional activity that assesses the learner's suspected problem.
3. Document the steps the learner follows to complete the activity (Step 2).
4. Construct a checklist that contains the sequence the learner follows; the teacher completes this checklist while observing the student engaged in the selected assessment activity.
5. Construct a self-analysis checklist similar to the checklist developed in Step 4.
6. Ensure that the instructional activity contains the steps and sequences necessary to assess the learner's area of suspected need; implement activity with learner.
7. Observe the student engaged in the activity; complete the teacher observation form and have the learner complete the self-analysis checklist upon completion of the task.
8. Analyze both checklist results and decide the extent to which the activity assessed needed skills and if the sequence assisted the learner to successfully complete the task.
9. If necessary, select and implement a new strategy; ensure that the learner follows the proper steps and sequence to complete the new strategy; complete checklists.
10. Plot the student's performance to monitor progress and illustrate growth in acquired knowledge and skills learned through completion of the selected instructional activity(ies) following the steps in the proper sequence (Collier & Thomas, 1989).

It is essential that only one element be changed at a time so the instructional element or activity producing a change is clearly identified. The intervention strategies used in analytic teaching assessment should also teach diverse learners how to employ higher-order thinking necessary to complete more complex tasks within culturally relevant contexts. The documentation of student performance, particularly those acquiring English as a second language, in the use of higher-order skills provides additional evidence-based documentation to problem-solving teams. Due to its combined and interrelated emphasis on instruction and associated monitoring of progress, analytic teaching results are highly useful in identifying the diverse learner's needs and in helping to differentiate learning differences due to cultural and linguistic diversity from a disability intrinsic within the student.

■ *Differentiating Difference from Disability.* Analytic teaching is a highly effective assessment practice for use with diverse learners because educators can select tasks and their implementation in culturally responsive ways. Accommodation of learning differences, preferred styles for learning, use of higher-order thinking skills, consideration of the needs of second language learners, or incorporation of cultural values in teaching and learning may occur through analytic teaching while specific learner needs in academic or social-emotional areas are assessed. Additionally, use of analytic teaching provides educators who are responsive to cultural diverse needs the opportunity to make individual decisions within an appropriate cultural context. (See Form 5.2, Guide for Implementing Culturally Responsive Analytic Teaching.)

Interviews

Overview

Interviews completed with the teacher, student, family members, or significant people from the community may serve as a valuable assessment practice to best understand the student's cultural values and norms. Interviews may also serve as an important practice to identify or clarify the diverse learner's educational and social needs (Stefanakis, 1998).

■ *Relevant Uses.* The interviewer must be sensitive to and knowledgeable about cross-cultural communication for interviews to be relevant. Figueroa and Newsome (2004) and Damico, Cheng, Deleon, Ferrer, and Westernoff (1992) identified the following important items that effective cross-cultural interviews may obtain:

1. Factors that affect and explain test performance (e.g., family, community, classroom setting).

2. Input from significant people in the learner's life (interviewed in their native language).

3. Greater understanding of student uses of both native language and English in the home and community, specifically oral language and literacy proficiency in both languages.

4. Determination of the primary instructional language used by educators and its compatibility with the learner's most proficient language.

■ *Steps/Process.* To facilitate an effective cross-cultural interview, Form 5.3 poses various questions that address areas and items important to interpreting assessment data within the context of the learner's cultural values, norms, and teachings.

■ *Differentiating Difference from Disability.* Interviews with the learner's teachers, parents/family, community members and peers provide valuable information about cultural values and norms that may assist the problem-solving team to better understand certain behaviors, such as those discussed in Chapter 3. Interview data assists to interpret assessment results or classroom behaviors within a relevant cultural context; a context that reflects diverse needs resulting in learning differences. This information can reduce the misinterpretation of various behaviors as disorders when, in reality, they reflect cultural values and teachings. (See Form 5.3, Guide for Conducting an Effective Cross-Cultural Interview, which was developed from discussions about interviews for diverse learners as found in Hoover et al. [2008].)

Language Sampling

Overview

Collection of language samples is a practice that has valuable assessment implications because learners demonstrate orally or in writing their use of language. This is a highly effective assessment practice that supports formal standardized language assessment (Hammill, 1987).

■ *Relevant Uses.* When used in the overall comprehensive assessment process, periodic language sampling provides authentic examples of oral and written language usage within a cultural context, providing valuable information needed to discern a learning difference from a disability.

■ *Steps/Process.* When collecting and analyzing oral or written language samples:

1. Be sure to collect them within several different language contexts.
2. Involve a familiar and culturally appropriate conversational partner for oral samples.
3. Provide a relaxed environment.
4. Audio and/or videotape language samples for later review by educators or problem-solving teams (typically requires written parental permission).
5. Solicit oral and written language samples in both language function (communicative, academic) and form.
6. Use caution if comparing language sample results to oral/written results obtained from commercially published and normed language tests (Baca & Cervantes, 2004; Hammill, 1987).

■ *Differentiating Difference from Disability.* Gathering, recording, and evaluating authentic oral and written language samples in the learner's native language and in English is an effective assessment practice. Writing samples may also be generated through journal responses that allow learners to reflect on or describe various topics or abilities: aspects of a story; personal successes or ideas; prior knowledge and experiences related to new learning; or different ways to illustrate use of higher-order thinking such as analysis, comprehension, evaluation, or synthesis (O'Malley & Pierce, 1996). Information and data gathered from language sampling over time may be charted to document growth or progress in language use (e.g., increased vocabulary, consistent use of higher-level thinking abilities, and reduction in writing errors). This information, in turn, may be used by problem-solving teams to better understand the relationship between academic or behavioral performances and language usage, relative to culturally diverse values and second language acquisition stages of development. Form 5.4, Guide to Identifying Student Use of Linguistic Features, developed from content found in Abedi (2004) and Hoover and Méndez Barletta (2008), can be used to determine how a learner uses selected important English linguistic features.

Observations

Overview

Observation of students in actual and authentic learning situations provides invaluable information necessary to complete a comprehensive assessment of diverse learners (Stefanakis, 1998; Wilkinson, Ortiz, & Robertson-Courtney, 2004). Classroom observations provide corroborating evidence to support, refute, or further clarify data gathered from other assessment practices. Checklists, guides, or running records should be used to accurately record the teacher's observations, which are then shared with the problem-solving team at a later time.

■ *Relevant Uses.* Observations provide the opportunity to determine the extent to which: (1) suspected problems are exhibited; (2) cultural and linguistic diversity is valued and incorporated into instruction; (3) instructional and learning style preferences between teacher and student are compatible; and (4) the suspected problem may be due to second language development needs, acculturation, or related cultural/linguistic factors. To be most effective, the observer must be sensitive to and knowledgeable about the student's culture and speak the primary language of instruction.

■ *Steps/Process.* The observer must:

1. Ensure that adequate time to fully complete the observation exists.
2. Select an activity or period of time that targets the student's performance relative to the suspected problem.

3. Document the content, interventions, interactions, and setting associated with the observation through the use of guides, checklists, or running records.

4. Focus on evidence of diverse needs exhibited and the manner with which these needs are being addressed.

5. Summarize and relate the observation to results obtained through other assessment practices.

■ *Differentiating Difference from Disability.* Observations of diverse learners in various educational settings (e.g., small-group instruction, peer interactions, during transition or other unstructured times) allow educators to collect information about how cultural and linguistic factors may influence or impact academic and social-emotional behaviors. Formal assessment devices provide quantitative data; observations provide qualitative evidence of authentic behaviors, which allow problem-solving teams to interpret more accurately learning or behavior differences resulting from cultural or linguistic needs rather than disability needs. See Form 5.5, Guide for Conducting Culturally Responsive Classroom Observations, which was developed from information found in Tharp (1997) and Hoover et al. (2008).

Review Existing Records

Overview

Educational records (when current, complete, and accurate) provide insight into a student's instructional history, especially given the high mobility of students in today's schools. Although in many situations the records are often inconsistent or incomplete, they may still contain some useful information particularly related to cultural values and norms that may have been erroneously misinterpreted by previous educators as evidence of disabilities.

■ *Relevant Uses.* Existing educational records provide information about the learner from the perspectives of both current and previous teachers and educators. Patterns of learning, prior instructional interventions, prior assessment results, or identified suspected learning or behavior problems may be found in educational records. These and similar types of information may be of use to problem-solving teams to help fill in gaps or understand previous educational efforts provided to the student.

■ *Steps/Process.* An accurate review of the records may easily be accomplished for diverse learners if educators know what specific types of information are needed. Form 5.6 lists the necessary and relevant information that can be gathered from existing records, which can then be used as one assessment practice to put learner needs in context.

■ *Differentiating Difference from Disability.* Review of existing educational records may provide valuable information to problem-solving teams as they attempt to determine whether a learning difference or a disability exists. If the type of information found on the guide is not available in the student's records, then other sources (e.g., siblings, parents, or other community members) need to be identified and consulted to secure this information. Differentiating learning differences from disabilities in diverse students cannot be accurately completed without information related to the items on the guide. This information is essential to understanding learner needs so that these needs can be placed in the proper cultural and linguistic context. As previously emphasized, lack of knowledge of these important learner characteristics is a "red flag" to problem-solving teams, and decisions related to suspected disabilities cannot be made until this information has been gathered and considered relative to the academic and/or behavior needs. (See Form 5.6 for a guide to review student records. The form was developed from discussions about review of records for diverse learners found in Hoover [2008], Hoover et al. [2008], and Wilkinson, Ortiz, and Robertson-Courtney [2004].)

Work Sample Analysis

Overview

In addition to written and oral language samples, work sample analysis is an assessment practice that collects, analyzes, charts, and summarizes student work in various content areas. Work sample analysis may be used as a means to chart progress over time in suspected areas of need for struggling learners.

■ *Relevant Uses.* Work samples may be gathered and analyzed in any area of instruction in which the learners produce, orally or in writing, some product or outcome. Work samples provide problem-solving teams with additional evidence about the ways in which students approach and complete tasks. Also, students' work samples provide authentic evidence to support, refute, or clarify data obtained from formalized testing, particularly since cultural or linguistic factors strongly influence student performance.

■ *Steps/Process.* Educators familiar with and sensitive to the student's cultural and linguistic background are best suited to perform and analyze the learner's work samples. The analysis process is simple to complete and may include use of formal guides or checklists that contain specifics related to the content area (e.g., steps followed to complete a math reasoning problem; factors to look for when analyzing proper sentence or paragraph structure; evidence of use of higher-order thinking abilities). Depending on the particular situation, analysis may be conducted on individual work samples or be completed on a collection of similar samples. However, the most critical aspect in the process of sample analysis is in the interpretation of that which appears evident, relative to cultural and linguistic factors such as stages of second language acquisition, community values or norms, influences of acculturation, or other behaviors discussed in previous chapters.

■ *Differentiating Difference from Disability.* Work sample analysis allows educators to study diverse learners' performance in different situations and attempt to interpret educational needs. Work samples provide authentic evidence of student abilities that can be put into a proper cultural context, necessary for problem-solving teams to make informed decisions about learning needs. Similar to other assessment practices, work sample analysis adds value to formal testing data by allowing culturally responsive interpretations to be considered to avoid misinterpreting a learning difference as a disability, which on the surface may seem evident from formal testing results.

Task Analysis

Overview

Task analysis is a technique designed to determine steps and prerequisites needed to complete a task (Hallahan et al., 2005). This evidence-based educational practice provides educators with clearly identified steps that students must master in order to acquire a broader skill comprised of those learned subskills.

■ *Relevant Uses.* When used as an assessment practice, task analysis provides information about a student's specific skill levels—both acquired and those needing mastery. It also provides a sequential process for acquiring skills and associated subskills, which may include necessary skills reflective of cultural or linguistic diverse needs (i.e., second language acquisition, acculturation, preferences to learning). Educators can personalize structured learning in culturally responsive ways and the documented results can then be shared with problem-solving teams.

■ *Steps/Process.* Once benchmarks have been identified, several steps make use of task analysis a successful classroom assessment practice for diverse learners (Hoover et al., 2008). These steps are:

1. *Identification.* Determine specific skills/subskills needed to facilitate achievement of the objective; list individual steps to follow to achieve the objective.

2. *Introduction.* Determine learner's prior knowledge/skills possessed in both native language (L1) and English (L2) (i.e., activation of prior knowledge).

3. *Modeling.* Desired skill/content is modeled using problem solving and direct instruction.

4. *Guided Practice.* Provide the learner meaningful opportunities to practice the skill or to use the content in a variety of ways with direct teacher support (e.g., scaffolding).

5. *Student Feedback.* Learners describe either in writing (journaling) or orally what they are thinking, doing, and learning as they engage in a specific task.

6. *Independent Practice.* Provide reduced teacher direction to students so they more independently demonstrate the skill or use the content in varied ways.

7. *Assessment Review.* Record student performance during each step, documenting what is observed, discussed, and learned as the student engages in the learning task (p. 155).

■ *Differentiating Difference from Disability.* Task analysis provides many diverse students with the guidance they need, particularly if they are less familiar with school expectations due to limited experiential background. In addition, task analysis activities reinforce the language skills the student has mastered and make apparent which skills are needed to develop further second language acquisition. Task analysis allows educators to break down learning in ways consistent with cultural values and teachings to determine if suspected needs are a result of different expectations or an intrinsic disorder within the student.

Curriculum-Based Measurement

Overview

Curriculum-based measurement (CBM) is an evidence-based strategy for measuring student progress in a systematic way using simple and valid measures. Research on the effects of CBM shows positive impacts on student achievement, particularly with students who have disabilities (Allinder, Fuchs, & Fuchs, 2004). Its implementation is also highly conducive to meeting diverse needs in the classroom and assessment process.

■ *Relevant Uses.* CBM includes provisions for charting data of student progress and, therefore, is a highly effective method for on-going progress monitoring of response to intervention. CBM informs educators of instructional effectiveness and serves as a foundation for generating benchmark goals in various academic areas.

■ *Steps/Process.* Various authors have discussed steps or procedures for implementing CBM (Allinder, Fuchs, & Fuchs, 2004; Hosp, Hosp, & Howell, 2007; Smith, Polloway, Patton, & Dowdy, 2004). Since CBM is criterion-referenced, it provides educators greater capacity to focus on necessary instructional changes and allows for classroom-specific procedures to be used that directly link instruction with assessment. The following example lists the tasks to include to properly conduct CBM. These were developed from discussions about CBM in the sources cited previously. For other examples of CBM procedures, the reader is referred to the sources cited in this section, as well as Deno and Fuchs (1987). CBM includes, at minimum, the following:

1. Gather necessary instructional materials.
2. Gather or develop brief tests (e.g., two- to three-minute assessments that are locally developed or commercially provided) that assess targeted skill(s).
3. Administer brief test, score, and chart results (administer on established schedule such as three times per week for six weeks).
4. Use initial score or an average of the first three scores as baseline data.
5. Compare subsequent scores to baseline score to determine progress.
6. Adjust classroom instruction based on student progress (i.e., if adequate progress is made continue with the instruction; make relevant changes as necessary should learner make insufficient progress).
7. Continue implementation of CBM throughout the school year, charting progress data and making instructional decisions based on the charted results.

While the manner in which educators may conduct CBM may vary across schools and classrooms, a most important aspect is that CBM be implemented in a standardized manner to ensure validity of process and results.

■ *Differentiating Difference from Disability.* When used appropriately, CBM is as reliable and valid as most standardized tests (Hammill & Bartel, 2004), and as a result, is of significant value as an assessment practice for diverse learners. Specifically, CBM is an alternative to the often biased standardized norm-referenced instruments discussed previously. The use of CBM assists with culturally responsive assessment in several ways:

1. Annual curricular benchmarks, appropriate for diverse learners, are easily identified and measured.
2. Progress toward the benchmarks are assessed, systematically and regularly, through short, culturally appropriate tests.
3. Brief tests are administered following standardized procedures, thereby increasing the reliability and validity of the progress monitoring.
4. Results facilitate direct differentiation of interventions occurring immediately if the student demonstrates inadequate progress, thus improving the possibility of implementing instruction that more directly reflects the learner's cultural and linguistic needs.

The implementation of CBM provides educators with regular opportunities to determine the effects of selected interventions on diverse learners' progress. If insufficient progress is made, instruction is modified, which may facilitate more appropriate implementation of culturally responsive education, especially if it was not initially provided in the classroom. In effect, CBM has the potential to help educators see firsthand the positive effects of accommodating diverse needs consistent with the student's level of second language acquisition, acculturation, preferred styles of learning, or other cultural and linguistic factors. In addition, problem-solving teams are provided charted data that is gathered on a regular basis, demonstrating student progress relative to culturally responsive education. With CBM results, teams can avoid misinterpreting progress-monitoring data as indicators of a disability as culturally responsive education is increased and progress is achieved.

Performance-Based Assessment

Overview

Performance-based assessment is an assessment practice in which student progress or performance is evaluated based on a constructed or generated product (Bender, 2002). The product may take many forms (e.g., poem, painting, essay, videotape) and may be of any length and depth provided it meets established performance criteria upon which the product is evaluated (i.e., scoring rubric).

■ *Relevant Uses.* In performance assessment, students demonstrate proficiency of knowledge and skills through the generation of real-world or authentic products (Bender, 2002). According to Lachat (2004), performance assessment challenges learners to use higher-order thinking and problem-solving abilities—something many educators deny diverse learners when they misinterpret learning differences as disabilities. Also, the scoring device (e.g., scoring guide; rubric) should clearly identify cultural relevancy reflecting cultural and linguistic factors based on diverse learner needs.

■ *Steps/Process.* Performance-based assessment for diverse learners includes the following characteristics and processes (Hoover et al., 2008; O'Malley & Pierce, 1996):

1. *Constructed Response.* Students construct or expand on a response; generate product.
2. *Higher-Order Thinking.* Students are challenged to use higher-order thinking skills in the response constructed.
3. *Authenticity.* Tasks are meaningful, challenging, and engaging and reflect real-world solutions.
4. *Integrative.* Performance tasks integrate language and other skills across content areas.
5. *Process and Product.* Strategies for generating the product are assessed as well as the final product or response.
6. *Depth vs. Breadth.* Assessment measures a student's depth of mastery of skills and breadth of knowledge.

This assessment practice is another opportunity for educators to facilitate culturally responsive assessment as an alternative to the often biased and limiting formal assessment devices.

■ *Differentiating Difference from Disability.* Performance-based assessment provides the opportunity for students to demonstrate skill proficiency associated with content knowledge commensurate with their stage of second language acquisition, acculturation, or other related cultural and linguistic factors. As a result, this assessment practice is highly personalized and allows learners to demonstrate knowledge, skills, and abilities in a manner consistent with their cultural values, interests, and teachings along with their level of second language acquisition. Problem-solving teams may use evidence from performance assessment as another source of information to best differentiate learning differences from disabilities. (See Form 5.7, Culturally Responsive Performance-Based Assessment Evaluation Guide, developed from information found in O'Malley and Pierce [1996] and Herman, Aschbacher, and Winters [1992].)

Running Records

Overview

Running records (Clay, 1993) is a form of miscue analysis that is easy to implement and interpret. Results from running records may be graphed over time to document and demonstrate reading skill development (O'Malley & Pierce, 1996).

■ *Relevant Uses.* A running record provides educators of diverse learners authentic information about basic reading skills exhibited through oral reading. It may be used to informally assess student reading abilities using both familiar and unfamiliar reading material.

■ *Steps/Process.* Running records are most appropriate for use with beginning and/or struggling readers (Clay, 1993). The general process to use running records is: "Using a blank sheet of paper, the teacher places a check mark for every word that is read correctly and records words the student reads that do not appear in the text" (O'Malley & Pierce, 1996, p. 124). Approximately ten minutes of text should be read by the student, without interruption (100–200 words), and various reading miscues are recorded, such as substitutions, omissions, hesitations, or self-corrections. Each word not correctly read aloud is recorded as one error unless it is self-corrected by the reader.

■ *Differentiating Difference from Disability.* Running records provide problem-solving teams with authentic and recorded data on oral reading miscues in beginning or struggling readers. This informal assessment practice is of value to diverse learners, especially second language learners, in that actual classroom performance is observed and documented, which in turn can be put into a relevant cultural context. In addition, educators can use running records to corroborate or further explain results from formal reading assessment devices. The fact that students are encouraged to read an entire passage without interruption is also important as it gives educators a more complete picture of the learner's reading abilities (O'Malley & Pierce, 1996). Running records data may also be charted over time to illustrate growth and response to reading interventions. These data help problem-solving teams avoid misinterpreting learning difficulties due to cultural/linguistic diversity from learning or behavior disorders.

Portfolio Assessment

Overview

Portfolio assessment is a process during which students compile a collection of work designed to illustrate their educational knowledge, skills, and growth. Portfolio assessment is a learner-centered approach that allows students input and ownership in their own learning (O'Malley & Pierce, 1996). While various types of portfolios exist, *assessment portfolios* are designed to reflect learning goals and provide the best opportunities for diverse learners to self-assess and evaluate their own progress within a cultural meaningful context.

■ *Relevant Uses.* Assessment portfolios have several relevant uses in today's schools, particularly for diverse learners. Students demonstrate both process and product in their learning as well as show their mastery of defined educational goals or benchmarks. Since portfolios include samples of student products, quality of work may be analyzed (Smith, Polloway, Patton, & Dowdy, 2004). In addition, assessment portfolios provide evidence of the problem-solving approaches or strategies the students may have used in their learning. Portfolios are effective tools for providing teachers insight into diverse learners' preferences for learning and aspects within education they perceive to be most relevant (e.g., culturally responsive tasks). A scoring rubric may be developed and used to evaluate the portfolio along with student reflections describing the significance of their selections. Each of these types of evaluation allows for cultural responsiveness both in process as well as product, which in turn increases the relevance of a completed assessment portfolio for diverse learners.

■ *Steps/Process.* The development of an effective *assessment portfolio* requires the collected efforts of both the student and the teacher. Together, the following items about the portfolio should be discussed:

1. Identify the purpose of the portfolio.
2. Clarify instructional goals and objectives.
3. Discuss types of authentic student work appropriate for inclusion in the portfolio (e.g., baseline work, draft copies of written work, self-reflections about progress, completed work, etc.).
4. Determine the process for collecting and organizing materials in the portfolio.
5. Agree that grading or scoring rubrics and checklists will be used to evaluate the portfolio.

6. Establish the self-assessment process and criteria.

7. Give support to learners who are initially unfamiliar with an assessment portfolio.

8. Create a timeline for portfolio completion.

9. Use completed portfolio (e.g., share at parent–teacher conferences, share with next year's teacher, facilitate student responsibility and accountability for own learning).

Overall, the use of portfolios with diverse learners facilitates growth toward assuming responsibility for own learning, self-evaluating own learning, and demonstrating on-going progress toward meeting defined goals or benchmarks in culturally responsive and relevant ways.

■ *Differentiating Difference from Disability.* The use of an assessment portfolio provides educators another authentic method for evaluating student progress while simultaneously allowing diverse learners to demonstrate growth in ways consistent with cultural values and norms. In addition, portfolios accommodate needs associated with second language development to ensure that learner differences are not misinterpreted as evidence of disabilities. By allowing diverse learners the flexibility to generate a relevant assessment portfolio, reflecting a meaningful cultural and linguistic context, educators value diversity in everyday teaching and learning and are provided tangible evidence from which to discern differences from disabilities.

Functional Behavioral Assessment (FBA)

Overview

Functional behavioral assessment (FBA) is a technique grounded in the idea that behavior serves some meaningful function for the learner (Durand & Carr, 1985; Webber & Plotts, 2008). In discussing student behaviors, Crone and Horner (2003) wrote that "people act the way they do for a reason" (p. 11). FBA clarifies suspected behavior problems, which in turn leads to more effective behavior interventions. This clarification is accomplished by identifying both the antecedent(s) and consequences to the behavior within the context of the learner's environment.

■ *Relevant Uses.* Functional behavioral assessment facilitates the assessment of behaviors in a way that considers environmental conditions relative to the behaviors. This procedure for assessing suspected behavior problems is highly relevant to diverse learners because consideration of the environment also includes consideration of cultural and linguistic factors that may influence the behaviors. Consideration of cultural norms and values in the identification and subsequent interpretation of behavioral needs reduces the possibilities associated with misinterpreting different behaviors, resulting from diversity, as disorders resulting from other concerns or learner issues.

■ *Steps/Process.* Operating from a generated hypothesis about the suspected behavior, problem-solving teams implement FBA by conducting interviews, direct observations, and review of student records (Crone & Horner, 2003). Once the behavior is clarified, effective FBA leads to the development of a behavior support plan (BSP), which includes selection and implementation of positive behavior supports (PBS) for meeting the identified behavior needs. (See Chapter 7 for discussion about PBS.) Completion of culturally competent interviews and classroom observations facilitates the implementation of a culturally responsive functional behavioral assessment.

■ *Differentiating Difference from Disability.* O'Neill et al. (1997) and Crone and Horner (2003) found that FBA was an effective assessment practice due to several factors: (1) both individual needs and environmental factors are considered in integrated ways; (2) behavioral interventions are more directly linked to the behavior; and (3) overall effectiveness in treating problem behaviors is supported by research. Through this process each of these three items will be more accurately determined for diverse learners who exhibit suspected behavior problems, due to an emphasis on environmental factors including cultural values and norms. The most significant aspect of FBA for diverse learners is that this process, if implemented in culturally responsive ways, assists to clarify differences from disorders thereby reducing misidentifying a behavior difference as a behavior disorder.

Assessment Accommodations

Perhaps the most significant feature in each of these assessment practices is that the educator can accommodate diverse needs to a point where the assessment accurately measures knowledge and skills within culturally responsive educational practices. Through appropriate accommodations, many of the biases previously discussed are confronted and reduced, which more accurately illustrate learner needs—both differences and disabilities. Without necessary accommodations to address diverse needs, problem-solving teams can only hope that the biases do not exist and trust that the assessment process is valid for diverse learners. However, we are past the time of "hope and trust" upon which to base critical decisions, and need to be held accountable for confirming with data and documentation that the assessment of diverse learners is in fact culturally responsive. Along with the assessment practices described here, an important aspect of ensuring appropriate assessment for diverse learners is to provide necessary accommodations to meet cultural and linguistic needs and reduce bias.

Accommodations are modifications made to the assessment environment to allow learners greater opportunity to be successful. Accommodations do not alter the goals or objectives of the assessment; rather, conditions within the assessment are adjusted to meet specific needs. Hoover et al. (2008) wrote, "it is important to bear in mind that accommodations are designed to alter conditions for assessment due to needs, which do not change the standards or benchmarks being assessed" (p. 155). If properly used with students who may be at a disadvantage due to level of English language development, limited experiential background or a disability, accommodations contribute to more appropriate learner opportunities to complete the assessment successfully. To ensure the most valid results when assessing diverse learners, the following types of accommodations may be necessary to implement.

1. *Presentation.* Adjusting how material is presented; assessment may require more or less visual or auditory emphasis

2. *Response.* Method of response is modified; assessment may require alternate response modes to accommodate diverse values and norms and language acquisition levels

3. *Time.* Time allotments are adjusted; more time to complete the assessment may be required due to needs associated with a language difference

4. *Scheduling.* Restructuring test-taking schedule; language needs may require adjustments to assessment schedules

5. *Setting.* Alter the location where student completes testing; assessment location in the school or classroom may need to be changed due to language needs or acculturation levels (Hoover et al., 2008, p. 155)

While these five accommodations are typically implemented for use with standardized or standards-based assessments designed to determine grade level or mastery proficiency levels, they may easily be incorporated into any of the assessment practices discussed in this chapter. As the various assessment practices are implemented, along with appropriate accommodations, problem-solving teams are provided culturally responsive assessment results, which advances the team's ability to avoid misinterpreting cultural and linguistic learning differences as learning or behavior disorders.

Concluding Thoughts on Culturally Responsive Assessment Practices

One of the underlying motivations for writing this book lies in my experiences with K–12 diverse learners and their teachers over the past three decades, where problem-solving teams consistently use biased or invalid assessment devices and procedures to evaluate students from culturally and linguistically diverse backgrounds. One major reason expressed as justification or rationalization for misinterpreting or misdiagnosing diverse needs as disabilities is the perception that few assessment practices exist to accurately assess diverse students in culturally responsive ways. Additionally, as we move into the multi-tier instruction and response to intervention structure for educating all learners, a more culturally responsive assessment process must be implemented. The assessment practices and accommodations discussed in this chapter are not new; however, they are often unused. Educators who wish to reduce the pervasive misinterpretation of diverse learners' skills and abilities as learning or behavior disorders must implement these assessment practices since they are particularly relevant to assessing learners within the context of culturally responsive education.

SUMMARY

This chapter has presented twelve selected proven practices that facilitate the implementation of a culturally responsive assessment for diverse learners. Each assessment practice was discussed relative to its specific implications for use in meeting culturally and linguistically diverse needs as the identified steps or processes are implemented. In addition, five highly useful accommodations to assist with both formal standardized/standards-based assessment and the various assessment practices discussed in this chapter were presented. Collectively, these assessment practices provide problem-solving teams with much information to make informed decisions about a learner's needs relative to cultural and linguistic diversity.

▶ Additional Activities to Support Learner Outcomes

1. Evaluate your school's problem-solving team to determine current practices used to ensure that learning differences are not misinterpreted as disabilities.

2. Generate a matrix that illustrates the various assessment practices used by your school's problem-solving team.

3. Describe how the use of one selected assessment practice may have assisted in further clarifying a learner's needs relative to cultural and linguistic diversity.

4. Develop a comprehensive plan for addressing various cultural and linguistic factors in a culturally responsive assessment process that facilitates differentiating learning differences from learning or behavior disabilities by implementing the selected assessment practices.

FORM 5.1 Guide to Non-Discriminatory Implementation of Assessment Practices

Instructions: Check each item, if appropriate, to record its use with the selected assessment practice to ensure cultural responsiveness. Indicate NA if item is not relevant to the assessment practice. Provide comments to clarify item as applied to learner.

Assessment practice for which this guide is completed (check one):

____ Analytic Teaching	____ Interviews	____ Language Sampling
____ Observations	____ Review Records	____ Work Sample Analysis
____ Task Analysis	____ CBM	____ Performance-Based Assessment
____ Running Records	____ Portfolio Assessment	____ FBA

Within the implementation of the selected assessment practice the following are included:

____ Cross-cultural values are evident in assessment practice.
Comments:

____ Information from the home and family setting is gathered to corroborate assessment/progress-monitoring data gathered through the assessment practice.
Comments:

____ Influences of acculturation variables on the at-risk needs are considered when implementing the assessment practice.
Comments:

____ Assessment practice is completed by culturally competent/proficient persons.
Comments:

____ Assessment practice includes consideration of linguistic goals when interpreting assessment results.
Comments:

____ Cultural values/norms are integrated into the implementation of the assessment practice.
Comments:

____ Assessment practice is completed in student's primary language and/or English if bilingual.
Comments:

____ If necessary, translators/interpreters are properly used to implement the assessment practice in culturally responsive ways.
Comments:

____ Assessment practice reflects sufficient opportunities to learn the knowledge/skills assessed.
Comments:

____ Assessment practices are authentic reflecting second language acquisition and culturally diverse needs.
Comments:

Instructions: Check each step in the analytic teaching activity to document completion of the item. Below each item, clarify the manner in which the item is culturally responsive, if necessary.

Specific Skill Area Emphasized: _____

_____ Baseline performance of current ability is determined.
Evidence of Cultural Responsiveness:

_____ An evidence-based intervention to be tested with the student is identified.
Evidence of Cultural Responsiveness:

_____ All main steps that must be completed in the intervention are documented.
Evidence of Cultural Responsiveness:

_____ An evaluation checklist is constructed identifying proper sequence student must follow to complete the steps in the intervention (teacher and student checklists).
Evidence of Cultural Responsiveness:

_____ Learner is engaged in the selected evidence-based intervention; student is observed and data recorded regarding performance relative to the content area addressed.
Evidence of Cultural Responsiveness:

_____ Teacher and student complete their evaluation checklists.
Evidence of Cultural Responsiveness:

_____ Results are compared and charted.
Evidence of Cultural Responsiveness:

_____ Decision concerning effectiveness of selected intervention is made; alternate intervention is selected if necessary.
Evidence of Cultural Responsiveness:

_____ Complete the above steps with new intervention (if selected).
Evidence of Cultural Responsiveness:

_____ Continue to use intervention with student, complete checklists to monitor progress, and chart results.
Evidence of Cultural Responsiveness:

_____ Monitor use of selected evidence-based intervention relative to student's response to the instruction and differentiate as results indicate.
Evidence of Cultural Responsiveness:

Interview Purpose: Discuss child's home life, school, and peer interactions with parent(s)/guardians

Instructions: Generate a question in the language and manner that elicits the most accurate responses from interviewees for the following topics:

Topic	*Response*
When family first arrived in this community	_____
Why family came to this community	_____
Description of home community	_____
Parents' line of work	_____
Family's adjustment to their new community	_____
Problems being experienced as they adjust to their new community	_____
Things family misses the most/least about previous community	_____
Things family likes most/least about new community	_____
Family's access to receiving needed medical/school services	_____
Preferred language(s) spoken at home by family members	_____
Preferred language(s) spoken at home by child	_____
How well child is adjusting to the new school	_____
Comparison of child's new school with previous schools attended	_____
Things child likes most/least about school	_____
Child's most/least favorite school subjects	_____
Person who helps your child the most with homework	_____
Child's success at making new friends in this new community	_____
Extent child spends more time alone in his new community vs. previous community	_____
Child's most favorite activity to do with friends	_____
Preferred language(s) child and friends speak while together	_____

FORM 5.4   Guide to Identifying Student Use of English Language Features

Teacher _____   Student _____   Date _____

Instructions: Rate the following to summarize student use of each linguistic feature in speaking and writing.

  1 = None (Exhibits no usage)   3 = Some (Exhibits regular but infrequent usage)

  2 = Infrequent (Sporadic, infrequent usage)   4 = Extensive (Exhibits regular and frequent usage)

To what extent does the learner use the following?

High-frequency English words found on high use lists

  Speaking   1   2   3   4
  Writing   1   2   3   4

Longer words (e.g., two to three syllables)

  Speaking   1   2   3   4
  Writing   1   2   3   4

Longer sentences with more extensive ideas

  Speaking   1   2   3   4
  Writing   1   2   3   4

Noun phrases that include several modifiers

  Speaking   1   2   3   4
  Writing   1   2   3   4

More extensive, longer question phrases

  Speaking   1   2   3   4
  Writing   1   2   3   4

Prepositions

  Speaking   1   2   3   4
  Writing   1   2   3   4

Proper syntax structure demonstrating knowledge of the relationships among sentences

  Speaking   1   2   3   4
  Writing   1   2   3   4

Subordinate clauses in sentences

  Speaking   1   2   3   4
  Writing   1   2   3   4

Abstract versus concrete examples/ideas

  Speaking   1   2   3   4
  Writing   1   2   3   4

Summary of language features most/least frequently used by the learner:

Student _____   Observer _____   Date _____

Content/Skill Area to Observe _____

Instructions: The items below reflect some of the specific practices or competencies considered important to implementing culturally responsive education. Using the scale below, indicate the extent to which the following items occur relative to the suspected area of need. *Comments for each item may also be recorded to further clarify the observation.*

 1 = None (No occurrences observed)

 2 = Infrequent (Sporadic, infrequent occurrences observed)

 3 = Some (Regular, infrequent occurrences observed)

 4 = Extensive (Regular and frequent occurrences observed)

To what extent do each of these occur during the observation?

1. Diverse cultural values/norms are included in lessons   1 2 3 4
   Comments:

2. Instruction is given in the student's most proficient language   1 2 3 4
   Comments:

3. Teacher scaffolds instruction   1 2 3 4
   Comments:

4. Lessons include a process for helping student activate prior knowledge
   and connect to previous personal experiences   1 2 3 4
   Comments:

5. Culturally responsive evidence-based interventions are used   1 2 3 4
   Comments:

6. Cognitively challenging tasks or discussions are provided   1 2 3 4
   Comments:

7. Students are engaged in cooperative learning tasks   1 2 3 4
   Comments:

8. Students are encouraged to use verbal dialogue   1 2 3 4
   Comments:

9. Students are encouraged to use functional language   1 2 3 4
   Comments:

10. Appropriate wait time for student response is provided   1 2 3 4
    Comments:

FORM 5.6 Reviewing Existing Records of Diverse Learners

Instructions: Check each item found in the review of records. Record the information found in the records.

Record Item   *Records Content*

Home and Community Cultural Values/Norms

____ Each language spoken at home   _____

____ Current level of student's English language
proficiency   _____

____ Student's native language proficiency   _____

____ Student's cultural background   _____

____ Trauma experienced in homeland   _____

____ Recent physical health history   _____

____ Recent emotional health history   _____

Educational Experiences

____ Time (yrs/months) residing in U.S.   _____

____ Time (yrs/months) in U.S. schools   _____

____ Bilingual instruction received   _____

____ ESL instruction received   _____

____ Response to instruction in previous schools _____

____ Preferred instructional methods in the classroom _____

____ Level of interpersonal communication skills _____

____ Level of academic language skills   _____

____ Overall quality of previous education   _____

Social/Acculturation

____ Quantity of social interactions with peers   _____

____ Quality of social interactions with peers   _____

____ Evidence of acculturative stress adjusting to
new community   _____

____ Evidence of acculturative stress adjusting to
U.S. classroom environments   _____

____ Cooperative learning abilities/strengths   _____

____ Social interactions at school compared to
interactions in home/community environments   _____

FORM 5.7   Culturally Responsive Performance-Based Assessment Evaluation Guide

Student _____   Teacher _____   Date _____

Instructions: Check each item as it relates to the student's constructed response. Space for documenting evidence within the product/response should also be recorded.

Name/Type of Constructed Response: _____

The learner constructed a response/product that . . .

_____ Is culturally and linguistically relevant to his/her values, experiences, and linguistic abilities
   Evidence:

_____ Demonstrates use of higher-order thinking abilities commensurate with linguistic abilities
   Evidence:

_____ Is authentic, reflecting challenging and cultural/linguistic values and previous experiences
   Evidence:

_____ Integrates language usage within other content areas
   Evidence:

_____ Utilizes a culturally meaningful process
   Evidence:

_____ Demonstrates both breadth and depth of knowledge in the content area addressed in the product
   Evidence:

Summary of skills and abilities the learner demonstrated by completion of the product/response:

Summary of evidence that illustrates cultural responsiveness in the learner's response/product:

CHAPTER 6

Bringing It All Together from Tier 1 through Special Education Referral

Ecological Framework to Meet Diverse Needs

▶ Significance to Contemporary Educational Contexts

As EDUCATORS WE MUST IMPLEMENT AN INSTRUCTIONAL FRAMEWORK that reflects the whole child if diversity needs are to be met through culturally competent or culturally proficient teaching practices. Neither assessment nor instruction operates in a vacuum; rather, the influences of one's community, home, as well as educational setting, are significant in shaping academic and social-emotional development and growth. As multi-tiered instruction and response to intervention services are provided to diverse learners, a more encompassing framework within which these occur (i.e., ecological) provides a broad-based structure for meeting a variety of cultural and linguistic needs in today's classrooms. This is significant since culturally competent or proficient assessment and instruction can only be achieved if the learner's total environment is understood and valued. Critical issues of today such as immigration, misdiagnosis of a disability, or inappropriate referrals of diverse learners to special education are best addressed using ecological principles applied to everyday instruction and assessment. Diverse learner needs may be more accurately identified and addressed if multi-tiered instruction and associated response to intervention practices are implemented within an ecological framework, due to its flexibility to account for various cultural and linguistic differences.

► Overview

The various concepts discussed throughout the book come together as problem-solving teams interrelate the ideas that best serve diverse learners and reduce misdiagnosing learning differences as learning or behavior disorders. Included in this chapter is a framework that emphasizes the ecological aspects of teaching and learning and how this framework facilitates the effective implementation of the total process of multi-tier instruction and response to intervention, which for some learners may result in a referral or placement into special education.

► Key Topics

- ► ecological framework
- ► culturally responsive multi-tiered learning
- ► culturally responsive prereferral interventions
- ► culturally responsive special education referral

► Learner Outcomes

Upon completion of this chapter, the reader will be able to:

1. Apply ecological variables in the problem-solving process to differentiate learning differences from learning or behavior disabilities.
2. Integrate multi-tiered response to intervention within an ecological framework.
3. Reduce use of biased decision-making practices in special education prereferral and placement.

INTRODUCTION

One of the realities within multi-tier instruction and associated decision-making based on progress-monitored response to interventions is that some diverse learners may eventually be considered for special education placement. As a result, whatever occurs through tiered instruction may ultimately be important information and documentation used in a formal referral for special education and subsequent related decisions. Should a learner progress through the various tiers or levels of intervention and fail to respond adequately to those interventions, consideration for special education may result. Therefore, the interventions implemented in each tier may eventually be synonymous with prereferral interventions if a formal referral to special education occurs. As a result, implementation of culturally responsive multi-tiered/RTI education becomes essential if the teams are to avoid erroneously interpreting lack of response to intervention as somehow indicative of a disability, rather than the more frequently accurate conclusion of learning differences as we have discussed thus far in this book.

Multi-tiered response to intervention was covered in detail in Chapter 2 and the reader is referred back to that chapter if necessary. However, a brief summary overview of the three-tier process is provided here.

1. Tier 1 instruction occurs along with initial screening (i.e., universal screening).

2. Tier 2 interventions occur should initial screening indicate potential problems.

3. Tier 3 interventions occur if adequate progress is not made through Tiers 1 and 2 instruction.

4. Formal referral and possible placement in special education occurs if repeated attempts in Tiers 2 or 3 do not generate adequate progress toward goals and benchmarks (may include Tier 4 intervention depending on school district structures).

Ecological Framework for Implementing Multi-Tiered RTI

An ecological framework in education emphasizes the significant role of the total environment in teaching and learning. An ecological model views the importance of the various influences the environment has in meeting the educational needs of students (Bronfenbrenner, 1995, 1979). Within this framework, three ecological factors are addressed in interrelated ways to best understand and meet the needs of diverse learners. These are: (1) learner factors; (2) classroom factors; and, (3) home/community factors. Students from culturally and linguistically diverse backgrounds bring a variety of strengths and needs relative to each of these three ecological factors. Aspects of each of these three factors were discussed in detail in previous chapters. Table 6.1, developed from information found in Baca and Cervantes (2004), Hoover et al. (2008), and Klingner, Hoover, and Baca (2008), provides a collective summary of those discussions bringing these three ecological elements together into one operational framework.

As shown, an overview of the three ecological factors (learner, classroom, home/community) is presented. Examples of ecological significance of each factor and specific data-gathering practices are also discussed. Problem-solving teams should make use of all resources available in order to make informed decisions concerning learning differences and learning/behavioral disabilities. The

TABLE 6.1 Ecological Framework for Educating Diverse Learners

Ecological Factor	Ecological Significant Information	Suggested Data-Gathering Practices
Learner Characteristics		
Language	Most proficient language must be determined to best ascertain academic needs	Analytic teaching, running records, language samples
Acculturation	Stress associated with adjusting to a new environment must not be misinterpreted as emotional/behavioral disorders	Acculturation inventory, cross-cultural interviews/observations, curriculum-based measurement
Experiential Background	Prerequisite skills, abilities, and experiences are critical to educational success; these are embedded within cultural experiences	Family interviews, review of records, work sample analysis
Values/Norms	Diverse cultural values/norms are represented within most classrooms; recognizing these facilitates learning relevance	Cross-cultural interview, portfolio assessment, performance-based assessment
Higher-Order Thinking	Higher-level thinking abilities are essential to effective learning and must be facilitated in culturally responsive ways	Analytic teaching, task analysis, performance-based assessment, work sample analysis, curriculum-based measurement
Teaching/Learning Styles	Cultural and linguistic background, values, and norms influence preferred styles of learning	Classroom observations, task analysis, reciprocal teaching, analytic teaching
Classroom Characteristics		
Linguistic Competence	Functional use of language is essential to classroom success; competence in language use is directly connected to family and home ecological factors	Analytic teaching, performance-based assessment, work samples (language)
Learning within Context	The context of the home, family, and community is reflected in student learning and class experiences should reflect these values	Classroom observations, cross-cultural interviews, task analysis, performance-based assessment
Cooperative Productivity	Engaging students and teachers in joint classroom activities facilitates on-going conversation while also allowing teachers to value the cultural norms of the student	Reciprocal teaching, scaffolding, task analysis, peer tutoring
Instructional Conversation	The on-going verbal interactions among teachers, students, and peers facilitate functional language use and development	Reciprocal teaching, peer tutoring, task analysis, performance-based assessment
Challenging Curriculum	Various ecological variables influence the relevance of education, which is reflected in the use of challenging curriculum facilitating student use of higher-level thinking skills	Journaling, work sample analysis, performance-based assessment, curriculum-based measurement
Home-Community Characteristics		
Home Language(s)	Primary language(s) spoken at home; primary language(s) student uses in community needs to be determined	Home language survey, home visit
Adjustment to New Environment	How well students make new friends and adjust to new home environment directly affects learning	Cross-cultural interviews, home visit
Family Educational History	Previous school experiences and successes provide context to educational progress	Cross-cultural interviews, records review, home visit

various identified assessment practices are provided as examples of possible formal or informal strategies that problem-solving teams can use to gather the necessary information about diverse learners to meet desired outcomes and goals. An integrated view of these three ecological factors provides problem-solving teams with a relevant and necessary framework within which to operate as multi-tier instruction and RTI are implemented for diverse learners. On-going consideration of these three interrelated ecological factors is essential to accurately determine:

1. The most appropriate tier of instruction
2. Selection of culturally responsive, evidence-based academic and behavioral interventions
3. Extent to which assessment practices are implemented in culturally responsive ways
4. Learning differences from learning or behavioral disabilities
5. Whether a referral to special education is warranted based on problems intrinsic to the learner

Ecological Response to Intervention Decision-Making

As suggested, RTI decisions to determine the most appropriate tier for instruction are based on recorded progress-monitoring data, which is reflective of student's learning through evidence-based instruction (Vaughn & Fuchs, 2003). Two major underlying assumptions within this process are: (1) the utilization of valid and reliable assessment, and (2) the fidelity of implementation of the research-based interventions. However, even with fidelity of implementation and use of appropriate assessment, an additional critical element lies within the interpretive decision-making process for RTI (i.e., associated ecological variables). The concept of ecological or environmental factors influencing learning is not new (Carroll, 1963; Bronfenbrenner, 1995, 1979; Rhodes & Tracy, 1978), nor can these factors be ignored in the interpretation of RTI results. The importance of including various ecological factors in educational decision-making is that factors other than those within the student often contribute to academic and/or behavioral needs (Brown, 2004). *Culturally valid response to intervention can only occur if tiered instruction is implemented in culturally responsive ways, and this may only occur if educators incorporate the diverse needs and strengths found within and resulting from the student, school, and home/community factors comprising an ecological framework.* Stated differently, culturally responsive education must be conducted throughout instruction provided within each tier of learning to avoid the pervasive misinterpretations of the past (i.e., learning differences as disabilities).

CULTURALLY RESPONSIVE TIER 1 INSTRUCTION ■ Ultimately, the success of multi-tiered instructional programming for all learners begins with a foundation of high quality, core instruction that is implemented in the general education classroom along with effective progress monitoring. For diverse learners, this means that Tier 1 instruction must be: (1) culturally responsive, (2) implemented by culturally proficient educators, (3) evaluated using culturally responsive assessment practices, and, (4) differentiated based on decisions made by problem-solving teams knowledgeable of the impact of culture and linguistic diversity on education.

In reference to Item 1 (*cultural responsive education*), Klingner and Edwards (2006) wrote that teachers must possess "culturally responsive attributes" (p. 113) in order to effectively connect instruction with academic progress for diverse populations of students in their classrooms. In addition, Chapter 1 presented several practices or instructional suggestions that teachers should include in their classrooms to ensure the implementation of culturally responsive education. Also included in effective Tier 1 instruction is consideration of all of the items presented in Table 6.1 as well as those discussed in Chapters 1 and 3.

► **Implications for Problem-Solving Teams:** Teams must ensure that the three ecological factors (i.e., student, classroom, and home/community) are adequately and meaningfully addressed in daily classroom instruction. Lack of academic or behavioral progress may more accurately reflect the insensitivity to the cultural and linguistic diversity that students bring to the learning situation rather than problems with student skills and abilities.

In regard to Item 2 (*cultural proficient teaching*), this topic was discussed in detail in Chapter 1. As you may recall, culturally proficient teaching is acquired as teachers progress through various stages of development. The ultimate goal is to become sufficiently competent so cultural and linguistic diversity is genuinely valued and incorporated into curriculum and instruction. This includes abilities to utilize students' prior knowledge and learning, primary language, interests, and motivations (Klingner, Sorrells, & Barrera, 2007). Culturally competent teaching in Tier 1 instruction includes incorporation of these ideas as well as the various factors identified in Table 6.1, and is essential to making informed decisions if a diverse learner is not making adequate progress toward curricular benchmarks.

► **Implications for Problem-Solving Teams:** Teams must ensure that teachers implementing Tier 1 instruction for diverse learners possess a minimum level of cultural competence. If this is not evident, teams are cautioned to scrutinize Tier 1 progress-monitoring results as they may more accurately reflect lack of sufficient opportunities to learn rather than lack of academic or behavioral progress.

Item 3 (*culturally responsive assessment*), necessary to implement effective education for diverse learners in Tier 1, reflects the topics addressed in Chapters 4 and 5: culturally responsive assessment process and practices. As discussed, the primary source upon which decisions concerning how well learners are progressing is found in the progress-monitoring process and selected instruments and practices. As presented in Chapter 5, numerous assessment practices exist to implement culturally responsive assessment. These practices need to be implemented bearing in mind the various suggestions for making them culturally responsive to best monitor diverse learners' academic and behavioral progress.

▶ **Implications for Problem-Solving Teams:** Assessment that monitors learners' progress toward curricular benchmarks must be completed using culturally valid and reliable instruments and practices. If diverse learners are inappropriately assessed in Tier 1, problem-solving teams begin the process of sending the learner down a path that, in the past, has led to the misidentification of learning differences as disorders. Therefore, problem-solving teams must make certain that progress-monitoring assessment in Tier 1 is relevant and responsive to cultural and linguistic needs. Use of the assessment practices, processes and measures presented in Chapters 4 and 5, and summarized in Table 6.1, provide problem-solving teams with greater confidence that Tier 1 education for learners includes culturally valid assessment.

Item 4 (*culturally responsive differentiations*) reflects the practice within Tier 1 in which reasonable and expected differentiation to instruction occurs for all learners to help achieve curricular benchmarks. These differentiations, which may vary, are provided to all learners as a component of daily instruction. Tier 2 intervention is considered for those learners who do not make adequate academic or behavioral progress after being provided Tier 1, high quality core instruction using evidence-based interventions. This also includes use of acceptable differentiations. Therefore, as diverse students begin to struggle with Tier 1 learning, evidence-based instructional differentiations are selected and implemented followed by on-going progress monitoring. As emphasized throughout this book, *any* differentiations to instruction must also be culturally responsive or problem-solving teams run the risk of believing that lack of progress may be due to learning or behavior disorders, without regard for the various cultural and linguistic factors summarized in Table 6.1.

▶ **Implications for Problem-Solving Teams:** Teams must confirm and have a high level of confidence that instructional differentiations provided to diverse learners are culturally responsive and accommodate various needs such as acculturation, stage of second language acquisition, or preferences toward instructional styles. Similar to the other three items discussed to help ensure effective Tier 1 instruction for diverse learners, differentiated instruction must be appropriate to avoid misinterpreting learning needs as problems reflecting intrinsic disabilities.

CULTURALLY RESPONSIVE TIER 2 INTERVENTIONS ■ Education for diverse learners through Tier 2 is determined after the students have had sufficient opportunities to learn in Tier 1 and do not make adequate progress toward meeting curricular benchmarks. The level of intervention in Tier 2 is more intensive and designed specifically to supplement Tier 1 instruction (Hoover & Patton, 2008; Vaughn, 2003). Of specific concern at this level of instruction is that it is currently unclear as to the best approach or approaches for addressing Tier 2 needs of diverse learners (Klingner & Edwards, 2006). Although questions remain concerning the differences between Tier 1 and 2 interventions (Speece & Walker, 2007), some practices are known and can be applied to meet the needs of diverse learners. Tier 2 interventions:

1. Are implemented in small groups.

2. Are designed to support or supplement Tier 1 instruction.

3. May be implemented in the general education classroom and/or in a pull-out situation.

4. Require more frequent progress monitoring than seen in Tier 1 (e.g., every two weeks versus three times per year).

5. Go beyond or provide additional exposure to differentiations begun in Tier 1.

▶ **Implications for Problem-Solving Teams:** Tier 2 interventions will only be effective and appropriate if they are based on culturally responsive Tier 1 instruction and associated progress monitoring. Since many of the evidence-based interventions have been researched with the general population of students, use of these will often require adaptations or modifications to best meet cultural and linguistic needs of diverse learners (Klingner & Edwards, 2006). This becomes significant to the decision-making process since problem-solving teams must be confident that Tier 2 interventions are selected and implemented in ways that do not conflict with cultural and linguistic needs and values (e.g., cooperative groups; longer wait times for a response; consideration of stage of second language acquisition; more structured learning environment). Otherwise, progress-monitoring results that show little or no progress toward benchmarks may be misinterpreted as a sign of a disability when in fact more culturally responsive, modified interventions may assist learners to achieve greater success. Similar to other aspects of tiered instruction and RTI previously discussed, problem-solving teams must be able to clearly demonstrate that at least two rounds of Tier 2 interventions and progress-monitoring assessment practices were sufficiently culturally responsive to address potential diverse needs. If these Tier 2 conditions are met and the students continue to make inadequate progress, they are provided more intensive Tier 3 interventions.

CULTURALLY RESPONSIVE TIER 3 INTERVENTIONS ■ At this point in the Tier instructional process, students are exhibiting more significant problems and have not responded to extensive interventions designed to supplement the Tier 1, core instruction. Also, it is at this point that students may be formally referred to special education while continuing to receive more individualized intervention that tends to deviate from the Tiers 1 and 2 curriculum. Speece and Walker (2007) wrote that Tier 3 intervention "is described as more individually focused and relying less on a standard curriculum, focusing instead on individual student needs" (p. 293). In reference to the education of diverse learners, all the same cultural and linguistic considerations discussed throughout this book must prevail to ensure that problem-solving teams make informed decisions about suspected learning problems.

▶ **Implications for Problem-Solving Teams:** By this time, learners should have been provided culturally responsive Tiers 1 and 2 interventions and had their progress monitored using culturally valid assessment devices and practices. Additionally, the problem-solving team has determined that these learners have not responded adequately to the Tiers 1 and 2 interventions and require additional, more intensive interventions and/or formal referral to special education. As discussed in the previous chapters, efforts and decisions made throughout the multi-tier process have had significant implications to diverse learners; however, for some learners a most critical decision point has now been reached: formal referral to and possible placement into special education with an identified disability (e.g., learning disability). For these students, this becomes significant and problem-solving teams must be very confident that culturally responsive education and response to intervention decision-making have actually occurred. If educators have successfully implemented the culturally relevant processes and practices, they will be able to make an informed decision concerning the possibility that a diverse learner may indeed have a disability. Form 6.1 provides a guide to determine the extent to which multi-tiered instruction is culturally responsive.

Culturally Responsive Referral Procedures

For some learners at this stage in the tiered process, the problem-solving team has decided that a disability may exist and that formal referral to special education is warranted. This action will begin the formal special education process and initiate procedural safeguards and rights afforded to all students through the Individual Disabilities Education Improvement Act of 2004 (IDEA, 2004). Therefore, the education received in each tier should provide sufficient assessment data to make informed decisions about a formal special education referral. To ensure the problem-solving team has relevant data to make informed decisions about diverse learners, Form 6.2, Checklist for Referral to Special Education of a Diverse Learner, developed from information discussed in Baca and Cervantes (2004) and Hoover et al. (2008), provides some key issues to address prior to initiating formal referral.

As illustrated on Form 6.2, a variety of issues such as determining language proficiency, meeting the parents, and conducting classroom observations should be documented prior to making a formal referral to special education. Should the items be sufficiently addressed and a formal referral be determined necessary, a review of some of the more critical issues to consider is warranted by the problem-solving team. These issues, developed from content in Klingner, Hoover, and Baca (2008) and Baca and Cervantes (2004), are illustrated in Table 6.2.

These comprehensive issues must be addressed to ensure that valid, meaningful, and culturally responsive referral and assessment practices are implemented for all learners within multi-tiered instructional programming.

TABLE 6.2 Critical Issues in Problem-Solving Team Decision-Making for Diverse Learners

Issue	Difference versus Disability Considerations
Second Language Acquisition, Cultural Values, Disability Characteristics	Second language acquisition and acculturation behaviors must not be misidentified for a learning or behavior disability
Evidence Based Interventions Precede Formal Referral to Special Education	Multi-tiered interventions must be implemented with fidelity by culturally competent teachers and culturally responsive progress monitoring must occur
Instructional/Assessment Language	Diverse learners must be instructed and assessed in their most proficient language
Limited English Proficiency and Intellectual Capacity/ Higher-Order Thinking	Limited English proficient abilities do not indicate limited intellectual functioning or inability to employ higher-order thinking skills
Sufficient Opportunities to Learn	Multi-tiered RTI must provide diverse learners with sufficient opportunities to learn as well as opportunities to demonstrate acquired knowledge and skills commensurate with second language acquisition stage of development
Culturally Responsive Observations and Interviews	Classroom observations and interviews must be conducted by culturally competent or proficient educators
Minimizing Assessment and Instructional Bias	Standardized test results must be corroborated with authentic, classroom-based culturally responsive assessment practices

SUMMARY

The tiered instructional process through which a diverse learner may progress begins with high quality Tier 1 evidence-based instruction, moves into supplemental Tier 2 interventions and, for some, results in intensive Tier 3 intervention, including possible special education referral and/or placement. Student progress is monitored to determine response to the interventions implemented, which is only as relevant as the interventions are at meeting interrelated ecological variables found within the student, classroom, and home/community. The integrated implementation of multi-tiered instruction and cultural responsiveness can best occur through consideration of the many diverse issues, practices, and concerns by problem-solving teams in today's schools. The ecological framework presented in this chapter ties together the many cultural and linguistic issues, no matter which Tier the learner is educated within. Implementation of tiered instruction and associated response to intervention progress monitoring for diverse learners must incorporate the ecological factors of student, classroom, and home/community, if: (1) appropriate referral to special education is to be made, and (2) proper decisions about learning differences versus learning or behavioral disorders are to be generated.

Additional Activities to Support Learner Outcomes

1. Conduct an evaluation of the extent to which the ecological variables associated with student, classroom, and home/community factors (refer back to Table 6.1) are incorporated in diverse learners' instruction.

2. Evaluate the extent to which your school implements culturally responsive multi-tiered instruction (Form 6.1).

3. Complete the referral checklist (Form 6.2) for a diverse learner who has recently been or is being considered for formal special education placement. Summarize the results to determine extent to which these items were addressed by the problem-solving team.

4. Document one example to illustrate how your school's problem-solving team addresses the critical issues summarized in Table 6.2.

Instructions: Indicate the extent to which the following occur as it relates to multi-tiered instruction using the following scale. Provide clarifying *Comments* as necessary for each item.

   1 = None (No evidence of occurrence)   3 = Some (Regularly but infrequently occurs)

   2 = Infrequent (Sporadically, infrequently occurs)   4 = Extensive (Regularly and frequently occurs)

To what extent do each of these occur?

____ Culturally responsive education in Tier 1 learning.   1   2   3   4
      Comment:

____ Cultural values students bring to the classroom are integrated into each Tier of instruction.   1   2   3   4
      Comment:

____ Cultural and linguistic diversity are accounted for in progress-monitoring assessments
      in each Tier.   1   2   3   4
      Comment:

      Cultural preferences are accommodated to match teaching with student-preferred
      styles of learning.   1   2   3   4
      Comment:

____ Evidence-based interventions containing research evidence showing effectiveness with
      diverse learners.   1   2   3   4
      Comment:

____ Three-tier instruction implemented by a culturally competent/proficient educator.   1   2   3   4
      Comment:

____ Instruction within multi-tiered learning provided in the student's most proficient language.   1   2   3   4
      Comment:

____ Interventions in multi-tiered instruction that are cognitively challenging to the student.   1   2   3   4
      Comment:

____ Numerous and sufficient opportunities to learn provided in Tier 1 prior to implementing
      subsequent tiered interventions.   1   2   3   4
      Comment:

Summary of extent to which multi-tiered instruction is culturally responsive:

Instructions: Confirm that the following were completed and addressed prior to initiating referral for special education. (Check each item as it is addressed.) Provide clarifying comments if needed. *Attach this completed form to the Reason for Referral.*

____ Most proficient instructional language is identified.
   Comments:

____ Alternative, authentic, or other classroom-based criterion-referenced assessments are completed.
   Comments:

____ Parent meeting is completed (e.g., home visit; meeting at school).
   Comments:

____ Teaching and student learning style compatibility is identified.
   Comments:

____ Sufficient opportunities to learn are provided to student.
   Comments:

____ Culturally responsive evidence-based interventions are implemented; results documented.
   Comments:

____ Language appropriate instruction occurs (i.e., ESL, bilingual instruction).
   Comments:

____ Acculturation level (e.g., adjustment to school/classroom environment) is determined.
   Comments:

____ Vision/hearing exams recently completed.
   Comments:

____ Culturally competent classroom observations are completed.
   Comments:

____ Response to intervention is monitored using culturally responsive assessment devices and practices.
   Comments:

Summary of culturally responsive reason for referral:

CHAPTER 7

Selecting and Implementing Evidence-Based Interventions

► Significance to Contemporary Educational Contexts

THE IMPLEMENTATION OF EVIDENCE-BASED INTERVENTIONS within multi-tiered instruction/RTI models has taken center-stage in K through 12 school systems. It is estimated that almost 20 percent of all learners in today's schools require some form of tiered, supplemental interventions based on documented response to evidence-based instruction implemented through the general education curriculum. Of particular concern to practitioners in today's schools are issues such as what exactly are the evidence-based interventions; how must these be implemented in the classroom; or to what extent can these be modified or differentiated while still keeping within the spirit of the intervention (i.e., implementation with fidelity). Educators may no longer use strategies based on personal preference; rather, they must select those that have been shown to be research based and effective in meeting the content and behavioral benchmarks identified in state- and district-mandated curricula.

Overview

The complex issues associated with evidence-based interventions with diverse learners at-risk are discussed. Topics covered in this chapter include the qualities necessary to consider in the identification and selection of evidence-based interventions, implementing these interventions with fidelity, and special considerations when selecting evidence-based interventions for use with culturally and linguistically diverse students. Examples of several evidence-based interventions are presented, including how these may be used effectively with diverse learners. Descriptions of evidence-based interventions and materials in the content area of reading are specifically emphasized due to their significance in differentiating learning differences from disabilities in diverse learners.

Key Topics

- ▶ evidence-based interventions
- ▶ implementation with fidelity
- ▶ direct instruction
- ▶ teacher developed scripted lessons
- ▶ scaffolding
- ▶ classwide peer tutoring
- ▶ positive behavior supports

Learner Outcomes

Upon completion of this chapter, the reader will be able to:

1. Articulate current issues related to the use of evidence-based interventions in the classroom.
2. Describe research practices followed to determine evidence-based interventions.
3. Articulate specific considerations when selecting and using evidence-based interventions with diverse learners.
4. Implement various evidence-based interventions and describe their effectiveness with diverse learners.
5. Articulate specific considerations for problem-solving teams to address to best use evidence-based interventions when differentiating learning differences from learning or behavior disabilities.

INTRODUCTION TO EVIDENCE-BASED EDUCATION

As discussed in previous chapters, differentiating learning differences from disabilities includes the application of knowledge and expertise in several areas: (1) multi-tiered/response to intervention, (2) ecological factors in teaching and learning, (3) culturally proficient teaching, and (4) culturally responsive assessment. In addition to these important qualities, the implementation of research or evidence-based interventions must occur. This topic was briefly introduced in Chapter 2 and will be further explored here. Within all tiers of instruction, teachers must select, use, and evaluate curriculum and pedagogy that emphasize structured, systematic, and direct approaches.

How Are Evidence-Based Interventions Identified?

Evidence-based interventions are strategies or materials that have been rigorously tested following specific research procedures, and demonstrate from this research effectiveness in meeting academic or behavior educational benchmarks. In 2002, the National Research Council identified six guiding principles for effectively researching educational methods or materials. In addition, Gough (2004) provided several stages to which researchers who synthesize collected research findings should adhere in order to generate the most valid results. Drawing from discussions from these two sources, the following summarized elements are considered essential to effective research, particularly scientific research. These discussions are specifically applied to research-based educational interventions and curriculum. These items guide consumers of evidence-based interventions/curriculum to determine, through review of the research, the extent to which rigorous research practices were applied:

1. Research identifies questions whose study will fill in gaps between current and desired knowledge, test hypotheses, or determining cause-effect relationships as related to teaching methods, curriculum, and educational progress.

2. Research is connected to prior studies through literature reviews and related/summarized with current evidence-based research results.

3. Researchers use a variety of quantitative and qualitative research methods to directly evaluate/assess the particular research question posed. While qualitative methods may be used, quantitative methods are preferred when testing evidence-based interventions.

4. Inferential reasoning skills are used to provide scientifically based research explanations, conclusions, and predictions about the effectiveness of a researched intervention. At the core of this practice is the development of a logical chain of reasoning to make informed educational decisions. Knowledge related to reliability, validity, bias, and ruling out other plausible explanations is also emphasized.

5. Once completed, the significance and importance of the research findings should be documented so others may replicate the research across settings. This ensures that evaluation and assessment of the effectiveness of curriculum and teaching methods may be used in similar ways with similar populations of learners in different types of classroom settings.

6. The significance of engaging in professional dialogue to discuss research and associated findings, relate results to previous research, and collaborate in decision-making are important to ensuring that effective educational interventions or materials may be used successfully in other settings with similar populations.

Form 7.1, developed from Hoover et al. (2008), Klingner and Edwards (2006), Moran and Mallot (2004), and Thomas and Pring (2004), provides a guide for ensuring that selected interventions are evidence or research based.

How Do Evidence-Based Interventions Assist with Effective Education?

Recent literature has outlined and discussed the significance of evidence-based educational teaching and assessment interventions to provide high quality instruction for all learners (Moran & Malott, 2004). Evidence-based interventions assist educators in meeting the following:

1. Determine learner progress toward clearly defined standards/goals.

2. Use empirical models of instruction in the classroom (e.g., direct instruction).

3. Differentiate instructional strategies when necessary.

4. Teach toward mastery of content and higher-order thinking abilities.

5. Directly and frequently measure growth toward curricular benchmarks (pre-post, repeated measures, ABA).

6. Generate explicit connections among outcomes, instruction and assessment. (Moran & Malott, 2004; Thomas & Pring, 2004)

If the evidence-based interventions are properly selected and implemented, they will assist educators to address these six items, which are essential components within multi-tiered response to intervention models.

What Does Implementation with Fidelity Mean?

Once the evidence-based intervention is selected, it must be used in a manner reflective of the process, procedures, and steps similar to the way it was researched and designed (i.e., fidelity). A highly effective intervention is only as beneficial to learners as it is implemented in the way it was designed to be used in the classroom. *Fidelity* of implementation is critical to ensuring that proper decisions are made relative to response to interventions. Problem-solving teams must be confident that the progress-monitoring results reflect properly implemented evidence-based interventions. A most effective way to determine that an intervention is implemented with fidelity is to have an educator other than the classroom teacher observe the instructional situation and complete a checklist the reflects effective teaching in the use of the selected intervention (NRCLD, www.nrcld.org). The types of factors that should be observed in assessing fidelity of implementation include pacing of instruction, use and availability of materials, presentation of the lesson or activity properly, scaffolding lessons if necessary, or management of off-task behaviors (Vaughn et al., 2006). Fidelity of implementation reflects quality teaching relative to and consistent with the manner in which the selected intervention is supposed to be taught in the classroom. Significant deviations from the established procedures in the intervention may yield inaccurate response to intervention progress-monitoring results and perpetuate misidentification of a learning difference as a disability for diverse learners.

What Special Considerations Exist When Using Evidence-Based Interventions with Diverse Learners?

As discussed throughout this book, determining learning differences from disabilities requires the problem-solving team to consider a variety of cultural and linguistic factors to best make informed decisions. Similar to the need to implement culturally responsive assessment and multi-tier/RTI is the need to implement culturally responsive evidence-based interventions. The following are items a problem-solving team should consider to ensure effective selection and implementation of evidence-based interventions with diverse learners:

1. Confirm that the implementation of evidence-based interventions has been completed with fidelity in cultural responsive ways.

2. Selected evidence-based intervention has been validated for its intended use (e.g., reading comprehension).

3. Selected evidence-based intervention has been validated with the population for which it is being used (e.g., struggling readers, English language learners).

4. Differentiated instruction occurs when necessary.

5. Progress-monitoring devices and procedures to assess the impact of the evidence-based interventions directly relate to the curriculum being implemented and are appropriate for use with diverse populations of learners.

6. Monitored progress associated with the evidence-based intervention is accurately recorded, charted, and interpreted within the proper cultural context.

7. Decision-making process accounts for expected variations in the implementation of evidence-based interventions necessary to accommodate second language acquisition needs and/or diverse cultural values, norms, and experiential background.

8. Confirm that the selected evidence-based intervention was sufficiently researched with populations of learners similar to those with whom it is used within the classroom.

Form 7.2 provides a guide for problem-solving teams to use to ensure that the evidence-based interventions are properly selected, implemented, and evaluated based on their intended purposes and researched populations.

Selected Evidence-Based Interventions

A variety of evidence-based interventions exist with varying degrees of supporting research. The following are several of these types of interventions, with a particular emphasis on reading interventions. These are not all-inclusive and are provided to demonstrate the types of interventions that exist along with discussion of relevance for use with diverse learners at-risk academically and/or behaviorally. For a more detailed coverage of existing evidence-based interventions, the reader is referred to the sources cited for each intervention discussed in the next section as well as the national website—*What Works Clearinghouse*—which identifies acceptable interventions for use with various learners including culturally and linguistically diverse students.

Descubriendo La Lectura

Descubriendo La Lectura is the Spanish version of *Reading Recovery* (Clay, 1985, 1993) providing short-term interventions in individual tutoring situations to learners in first grade who are at-risk in reading. When using this approach, students receive half-hour lessons on a daily basis for several weeks, ranging from twelve to twenty weeks. This approach is appropriate for assisting diverse learners who experience problems with reading and writing in bilingual classrooms.

► **Effectiveness with Diverse Learners:** Research suggests that this approach is best used with students whose reading or writing levels are somewhat below their peers, yet do not exhibit more severe reading problems. Neal and Kelly (1999) found that 75 percent of students using this method made sufficient progress while only 25 percent did not make adequate progress. Therefore, *Descubriendo La Lectura* has a research base illustrating success with first-grade learners in bilingual classrooms.

Read Naturally

Read Naturally is an intervention designed to increase student fluency (i.e., speed, accuracy, and proper expression). It is implemented for at least three, thirty-minute reading sessions each week. Use of repeated and connected text, vocabulary development, comprehension support, and on-going progress monitoring are included in this highly intensive form of reading intervention (Hoover et al., 2008).

► **Effectiveness with Diverse Learners:** *Read Naturally* using Spanish text was found to be effective at improving fluency, and to some degree, reading comprehension in first- and second-grade diverse learners who were struggling with reading (De La Colina et al., 2001). In addition, learners who were highly engaged in the *Read Naturally* process made the most progress, demonstrating further evidence of its effectiveness if implemented with fidelity.

Read Well

Read Well is a systematic, explicit phonics commercial program that emphasizes development of contextualized vocabulary, decodable text, and comprehension (Hoover et al., 2008). Designed for students in the elementary grades who lack reading fluency, *Read Well* provides learners with individual or small-group tutoring. The tutoring is implemented in 40-minute sessions for a period of ten weeks, three times per week where word identification, comprehension, and word attack skills are emphasized.

► **Effectiveness with Diverse Learners:** Effectiveness of *Read Well* was studied with struggling diverse readers in grades 2 through 5. When compared to those students who did not receive *Read Well,* Denton and colleagues (2004) found that diverse students learning English showed significant growth in word identification. As a result, *Read Well* has been shown to be an effective intervention for improving word-identification skills in English language learners in grades 2 through 5.

Reciprocal Teaching

Reciprocal teaching was originally developed for use with poor readers who struggle with comprehension (Palincsar & Brown, 1984). Through this method, students and the teacher collaboratively study a paragraph of written text through dialogue, think-aloud, and teacher modeling. The teacher guides the students to use four comprehension strategies found within reciprocal teaching: questioning, summarizing, clarifying, and predicating. Initially, the teacher helps the students with these comprehension strategies through modeling, scaffolding, and other guided practice techniques. Eventually, as the students implement and use the strategies more independently, gradual reduction of teacher assistance, support, and dialogue occurs.

▶ **Effectiveness with Diverse Learners:** *Reciprocal Teaching* has been shown to be useful with first language learners who are struggling with reading (Rosenshine & Meister, 1994). However, some evidence also suggests it is useful with second language readers who have comprehension difficulties (Klingner & Vaughn, 1996). More specifically, Fung and colleagues (2003) found that *Reciprocal Teaching* helped students use both first and second languages in acquiring improved reading comprehension of expository text. Additionally, Klingner and Vaughn (1996) found that this method benefited English language learners who had both decoding and comprehension needs in reading.

Classwide Peer Tutoring (CWPT)

CWPT is a reciprocal peer tutoring strategy that incorporates elements of cooperative learning into classroom instruction (Meese, 2001). Through a question/answer peer tutoring process that generally occurs two to four times per week in thirty-minute sessions the students take turns assisting each other in order to acquire knowledge and skills. This format increases students' active engagement and motivates them to learn the material (Meese, 2001). CWPT has been extensively researched and shown to be effective in improving academic performance in both elementary and secondary education (Allsopp, 1997; Greenwood et al., 2001; Reddy et al., 1999).

▶ **Effectiveness with Diverse Learners:** Research studies that focused on culturally and linguistically diverse students found increases in English language use and achievement through use of CWPT (Arreaga-Mayer, 1998). Also, the effects of the program titled *Peer-Assisted Learning Strategies* (*PALS*), a reciprocal classwide peer-tutoring strategy, was investigated by Saenz, Fuchs, and Fuchs (2005). These researchers found that PALS improves the reading comprehension of ELLs with and without learning disabilities.

Direct Instruction

One of the more long-standing educational interventions that has consistently shown to be effective in meeting a variety of needs is *direct instruction* (DI). According to Moran and Malott (2004), DI contains three important elements:

1. Scientific approach that identifies how curriculum and instruction should be organized and essential topics to be taught.

2. Integrated process that systematically teaches and develops academic and behavioral skills.

3. Specific procedures and practices that clarify how teachers and students should interact to best facilitate systematic and sequential learning.

Overall, direct instruction assists teachers to organize curriculum in such a way that knowledge, skills, and strategies are generalizable (Engelmann & Carnine, 1982). Examples of existing educational programs developed using DI principles include *Reading Mastery* and *Saxon Math*. Direct instruction in reading frequently includes the teaching of the most basic reading skills as identified by the National Reading Panel (2000). These include development of reading phonological skills, phonics, fluency, vocabulary, and comprehension.

▶ **Effectiveness with Diverse Learners:** The basic principles and structures provided to students through direct instruction are very relevant to diverse learners acquiring a second language and/or are experiencing difficulties with acculturation. Over time, DI has been shown to be a highly successful evidence-based intervention and been found to: (1) reflect effective instruction; (2) result in strong positive effects in learning; and, (3) be effective in meeting various needs associated with different student populations (which may include diverse learners), grade levels, and content areas (Moran & Malott, 2004).

Teacher-Made Scripted Lessons

An application of the direct instruction principles previously discussed can easily be applied to teacher-developed lessons and activities through a process termed *teacher-made scripted lessons*. "Scripted lessons" are teacher-developed explicit lessons that include several sequential steps: (1) presentation of new material, (2) guided practice, (3) modeling of proper steps and sequence, (4) informal initial assessment of the acquisition of new knowledge and skills, (5) independent practice, and (6) formal assessment of acquired knowledge and skills (Moran & Malott, 2004). This task analysis, explicit intervention provides teachers with another method for meeting diverse needs in the classroom.

▶ **Effectiveness with Diverse Learners:** Similar to direct instruction, teacher-made scripted lessons contain many qualities and characteristics that are of benefit to students learning a second language and those experiencing problems with acculturation or needed experiential background. Research has shown that students who are taught through this intervention spend more time actively engaged in learning along with associated increases in academic achievement (Rieth & Evertson, 1988). Additionally, Moran and Malott (2004) wrote that this intervention "can lead to lower levels of misbehavior and higher levels of achievement" (p. 106). The teacher's ability to put learning into a culturally responsive context also supports the importance of using teacher-made scripted lessons with diverse learners in any grade.

Personalized System of Instruction (PSI)

The *Personalized System of Instruction* (Keller, 1968) was originally developed as an alternative to college instruction. Its use with elementary and secondary students is important in that it reflects the principles associated with the evidence-based intervention known as *mastery learning*. According to Ormrod (2000), mastery learning is a systematic form of intervention that recognizes the importance of "mastering" basic skills and competencies prior to proceeding with the acquisition of more complex material. This mastering process provides the foundation for PSI in which the following elements are present (Keller, 1968; Moran & Malott, 2004):

1. Mastery of each unit must precede beginning the next unit.
2. Self-pacing determines how quickly the student progresses through the material.
3. Verbal presentation of material is completed for the purpose of demonstration only, not as the primary means of delivering content.
4. Students interact primarily with printed material in the learning process along with verbal interactions provided through supplemental tutoring.
5. Educators serve as individuals to administer assessments, provide constructive feedback, and provide supplemental tutoring assistance if necessary.

As mentioned, self-pacing occurs because different students learn at different rates and may require different amounts of time to master knowledge and skills. This is particularly relevant to diverse learners in the process of acquiring a second language and/or those who require additional time to respond to learning due to cultural or linguistic diversity.

▶ **Effectiveness with Diverse Learners:** Over the past few decades, numerous studies have been conducted to determine the effectiveness of PSI (Sherman, 1992). According to Moran and Malott (2004) most of these studies have concluded that PSI facilitates better acquisition of content and longer retention or material than traditional methods of lecture-type instruction. For students who are able to learn using self-pacing strategies, including diverse learners who possess sufficient language abilities, PSI provides an effective evidence-based alternative or supplemental form of intervention that is organized, explicit, individualized, and sequential in design.

Positive Behavior Supports (PBS)

Linked directly to functional behavioral assessment (FBA) discussed in Chapter 5 are positive behavior supports. The research base for PBS provides principles and practices that may assist educators of diverse learners to address social-emotional and behavioral needs reflective of cultural and linguistic diversity. This, in turn, helps educators avoid misinterpreting various behaviors as disorders rather than expected behaviors due to culturally diverse values, norms, and customs. According to Smith et al. (2004), positive behavior supports include a variety of interventions designed to increase positive behavior so as to facilitate students achieving goals in socially acceptable ways. The directed efforts toward reshaping the environment along with an emphasis on changing individual behaviors are of particular concern in the implementation of PBS (Horner, 2000).

These practices relate directly to the ecological framework for educating diverse learners as discussed in Chapter 6. Ecological variables associated with positive behavior supports include those related to the classroom environment, opportunities to learn, along with home and community factors. Therefore, as educators select PBS using information recorded in the functional behavioral analysis process, cultural and linguistic diversity must be considered to effectively implement interventions with diverse learners. A variety of educational interventions exists to support positive behaviors such as those found in Horner (2000), Smith et al. (2004), Webber and Scheuermann (1991), as well as Appendix A of this book. However, whichever support interventions are selected, they must reflect cultural and linguistic diversity for best results with diverse learners.

▶ **Effectiveness with Diverse Learners:** The emphasis on ecological factors to address diverse behavior needs relates directly to successful use of PBS with diverse learners. By considering the environment and its influence on student behaviors, cultural values, and norms may be more easily incorporated into the selection and use of positive behavior supports. Additionally, as diverse values, acculturation, experiential background, or second language acquisition behaviors are considered educators reduce the risk of misinterpreting *different* behaviors as *deviant* behaviors. Therefore, for diverse learners, effective implementation of positive behavior supports includes consideration of the various cultural and linguistic factors presented in previous chapters. Only through consideration of cultural and linguistic factors can PBS be effectively implemented for diverse learners, similar to that which is emphasized for selection and use of other interventions discussed in this chapter.

Scaffolding

Scaffolding is an intervention highly effective with diverse learners due to its emphasis on "simplified language, teacher modeling, visuals and graphics, cooperative learning, and hands-on experiences" (Ovando, Collier, & Combs, 2003, p. 345). Additionally, scaffolding helps to maintain a highly challenging curriculum for diverse learners without the effects of "watered-down" approaches often associated with the education of second language learners and those who exhibit culturally diverse needs. In particular, through scaffolding educators simplify language, use shorter sentences, provide brief directions as well as implement instruction using visual aids, graphic organizers or other useful tables and charts (Ovando, Collier, & Combs, 2003).

▶ **Effectiveness with Diverse Learners:** The effectiveness of scaffolding for diverse learners is described by Ovando, Collier, and Combs (2003) who emphasize the use of selected strategies previously discussed to assist second language learners in the classroom. In addition, Bender (2002) wrote that scaffolding is an effective form of intervention through the use of a sequential series of prompted content, materials, and support. Through guided instruction, all learners including culturally and linguistically diverse students, receive necessary supports and scaffolds to meet their individual learning needs.

Other Interventions

A variety of additional evidence-based interventions are briefly discussed here. Each of these has potential to benefit diverse learners who exhibit learning differences due to the acquisition of a second language and/or varying cultural values and norms. The reader is referred to the sources cited for each intervention for more specifics on the process and procedures needed to implement these with fidelity.

THE LANGUAGE EXPERIENCE APPROACH (LEA) ■ LEA utilizes a student's own language in the development of reading abilities (Allen, 1976). Within the LEA, students dictate a story which is written down, and then copy or trace what is written, illustrate the story, and read the story several times

(Hoover et al., 2008). This is a highly effective method for diverse learners because students use their own developed language in learning to read. For many years, LEA has been used successfully with emergent readers and can be implemented in various ways (e.g., with individual child, with a small group of children, or with an entire class). It may also be used successfully with learners acquiring a second language with or without disabilities (Haager & Klingner, 2005; Peregoy & Boyle, 2001).

WORDLESS PICTURE BOOKS ■ Use of wordless picture books is another motivating and effective method for helping diverse learners who struggle with reading (Peregoy & Boyle, 2001). The process is similar to that of LEA except the student dictates a story based on pictures viewed in a wordless picture book. It is appropriate for any age English language learner who is struggling with reading (Peregoy & Boyle, 2001).

COOPERATIVE LEARNING ■ Cooperative learning is a highly effective intervention when used with diverse learners including those with learning disabilities (Klingner & Vaughn, 2000). According to Johnson and Johnson (1993), cooperative learning benefits low-, average-, as well as high-achieving students. It is especially valuable to English language learners since they are exposed to more comprehensible learning by receiving adjusted language from peers within meaningful contexts (Kagan & High, 2002).

COLLABORATIVE STRATEGIC READING (CSR) ■ This intervention utilizes cooperative learning principles and reading strategy instruction (Palincsar & Brown, 1984) to improve comprehension (Klingner et al., 2001). "CSR has been used successfully in classrooms with culturally and linguistically diverse students at all achievement levels, ELLs who have learning disabilities, students with disabilities, as well as other students who are reading on or above grade level at both the elementary and middle school levels" (Hoover et al., 2008, p. 195).

READER RESPONSE JOURNALS ■ This intervention facilitates a student's recording of feelings, reactions, and impressions obtained through reading (Atwell, 1998). This process allows learners to become more engaged in their reading, improve comprehension, and further advance reading as a rewarding experience (Hancock, 1993). Based on reader response theory (Flood & Lapp, 1988), *reader response journals* allow learners greater opportunity to acquire more significant meaning from the reading experience that is put into a culturally and linguistically relevant context (Hoover et al., 2008).

THE COGNITIVE ACADEMIC LANGUAGE LEARNING APPROACH (CALLA) ■ CALLA was designed to assist diverse learners to use language to best integrate content with language (Winzer & Mazurek, 1998). It assists diverse learners to more effectively participate in inclusive class settings (Chamot & O'Malley, 1996). CALLA is best used with students at the intermediate or advance stages of English language development and includes five components: preparation, presentation, practice, evaluation, and expansion (O'Malley, 1988). Research has shown CALLA to be an effective evidence-based intervention with English language learners in the content areas of math and science (Galland, 1995; Thomas, 1992).

SUMMARY

The selection and use of evidence-based interventions appropriately implemented with fidelity for diverse learners is essential for determining learning differences from learning or behavior disorders. Each of the various evidence-based interventions discussed in this chapter has the potential to assist problem-solving teams to differentiate learning differences from disabilities within the parameters of multi-tiered/RTI models. Each of these research-based interventions facilitates valuable learning experiences if implemented in culturally proficient ways as discussed in the previous chapters. In addition, as ecological principles are addressed, learning and behavior needs of diverse students will be more accurately identified, leading to the selection and use of culturally responsive evidence-based behavior and academic interventions.

Additional Activities to Support Learner Outcomes

1. Evaluate your school's use of evidence-based interventions with diverse learners.

2. Use one of the evidence-based reading interventions with a diverse learner struggling with reading and determine how cultural values and norms are considered in its implementation.

3. Determine if perceived evidence-based interventions for use with diverse learners are in fact appropriate for the learner in question by completing Form 7.1.

4. Describe the ways in which your school's problem-solving team ensures that the selected evidence-based intervention is implemented with fidelity.

Instructions: Rate each item as it relates to the evidence-based intervention used with the learner using the scale. Provide clarifying *Comments* as necessary for each item.

Evidence-Based Intervention: _____

1 = Not Documented   2 = Documented to Some Extent   3 = Well Documented

To what extent does the documentation of the evidence-based intervention include . . .

1. Clearly defined and described purpose(s).   1   2   3
    Comment:

2. Research conditions/classrooms/settings.   1   2   3
    Comment:

3. Research with diverse populations similar to the student.   1   2   3
    Comment:

4. Evidence of effectiveness for its intended/stated purpose(s).   1   2   3
    Comment:

5. How to implement the intervention in a classroom similar to that in which it was developed and tested.   1   2   3
    Comment:

6. Effectiveness in a clearly defined school or field based setting.   1   2   3
    Comment:

7. Acceptable variations to accommodate diverse learner needs while still implementing with fidelity.   1   2   3
    Comment:

8. Replication of the intervention with similar populations to the student in various settings/conditions.   1   2   3
    Comment:

9. Evidence of how the intervention is culturally responsive to diverse learner needs.   1   2   3
    Comment:

10. Clearly defined characteristics of the population for which the intervention was tested and shown to be effective.   1   2   3
    Comment:

Summary of extent to which evidence-based intervention is well-documented:

Guide for Determining Appropriateness of Evidence-Based
Interventions for Use with Diverse Learners

Student _____ Teacher _____ Date _____

Evidence-Based Intervention: _____

Check each item as it pertains to the selected evidence-based intervention.

_____ Confirm that the implementation of the evidence-based intervention has been completed with fidelity
in culturally responsive ways.
Comments:

_____ Selected evidence-based intervention has been validated for its intended use (e.g., reading comprehension).
Comments:

_____ Selected evidence-based intervention has been validated with the population for which it is being used
(e.g., struggling readers; English language learners).
Comments:

_____ Differentiated instruction occurs when necessary.
Comments:

_____ Progress-monitoring devices and procedures to assess the impact of the evidence-based intervention directly
relate to the curriculum being implemented and are appropriate for use with diverse populations of learners.
Comments:

_____ Monitored progress associated with the evidence-based intervention is accurately recorded, charted, and
interpreted within the proper cultural context.
Comments:

_____ Decision-making process accounts for expected variations in the implementation of the evidence-based
intervention necessary to accommodate second language acquisition needs and/or diverse cultural values,
norms, and experiential background.
Comments:

_____ Confirm that the selected evidence-based intervention was sufficiently researched with populations of
learners similar to those with whom it is used within the classroom.
Comments:

CHAPTER 8

Culturally Responsive Collaboration in Tiered Instruction

Significance to Contemporary Educational Contexts

THE VERY NATURE OF MULTI-TIERED INSTRUCTION and use of problem-solving teams to make response to intervention decisions requires that educators collaborate to meet diverse needs. The process of educating a student across educational tiers by providing supplemental support and/or intensive intervention necessitates the need for a variety of decisions concerning issues such as differentiating instruction, accommodating diversity, or selecting and implementing culturally responsive assessment practices. This is significant in today's schools since, collectively, these and related areas reflect an enormous amount of knowledge, skill, and expertise typically not possessed by one individual. Collaboration among professionals, community members, and parents is essential to meeting diverse needs and for meeting the overall goal of avoiding practices that lead to misidentifying learning differences as learning or behavior disabilities.

▶ Overview

This chapter discusses collaborative roles and skills needed to meet the needs of diverse learners within multi-tiered instruction and response to intervention. Given the complexities and scope of needs exhibited by many diverse learners, various educational personnel are frequently necessary to assist with the identification, implementation, and evaluation of interventions. The effective implementation of tiered instruction, progress monitoring, and decision-making relative to response to intervention requires a team of educators who collectively possess the knowledge and skills discussed in previous chapters.

▶ Key Topics

- ▶ collaboration skills
- ▶ educator roles specific to RTI and multi-tiered instruction
- ▶ collaboration process for meeting diverse needs

▶ Learner Outcomes

Upon completion of this chapter, the reader will be able to:

1. Identify skills and abilities necessary to collaborate with other educators.
2. Implement roles effectively within tiered learning and RTI.
3. Implement a culturally responsive collaborative process.
4. Collaborate with other educators to advocate for the most appropriate education for diverse learners, including those at-risk and those with disabilities.

INTRODUCTION

Problem-solving teams need members who collectively bring a variety of abilities to the team including those who speak the students' and parents' most proficient language, understand the cultural values and norms the learner has been taught, are able to operate within an ecological framework, are well-versed in second language acquisition, and are able to implement and interpret culturally responsive assessment practices. Collaboration "emerges out of concerns by individuals who are like-minded in some ways and very different in others" (Walther-Thomas, Korinek, & McLaughlin, 2005, p. 183). This statement clearly reflects collaboration for diverse learners given the variety of needs and influences that different cultures have on today's classrooms. Collaboration includes several interrelated components including shared leadership, coherent vision, comprehensive planning, adequate resources, sustained implementation, and continuous evaluation and improvement (Walther-Thomas, Korinek, & McLaughlin, 2005).

Most schools currently have problem-solving teams in place to serve the needs of its learners and the importance of effective collaboration is generally understood by most educators. For our purposes in this chapter, we discuss selected aspects of collaboration necessary for problem-solving teams to best differentiate learning differences from disabilities for diverse learners. For a comprehensive coverage of collaboration the reader is referred to Friend and Cook (2003), Kampwirth (2006), and Walther-Thomas, Korinek, and McLaughlin (2005). We begin by discussing team membership necessary to successfully implement the problem-solving model previously described in Chapter 2.

Essential Members of the Problem-Solving Team

In order for problem-solving teams to effectively collaborate to meet the needs of diverse learners, the team must include key members. The knowledge and skills associated with the diverse cultural and linguistic needs discussed throughout this book are extensive and may appear overwhelming. As a result, to best address needs through culturally responsive tiered instruction in ways such as supporting general class teachers, implementing various levels of intervention, completing progress monitoring, accurately determining learner response to intervention, or formally referring a student for special education several educators must be actively involved. It should be clear to the reader why different types of individuals are essential to best meet diverse learner needs as summarized in the list that follows. Each of these types of individuals is identified along with specific contributions to the problem-solving team.

Type of Educator	Significant Multi-Tiered Team Contributions
ESL/Bilingual Educator	Provide knowledge about cultural and linguistic issues; put response to intervention results into a proper cultural context; clarify learning needs associated with acculturation, second language acquisition, or evidence-based interventions for diverse students; assist with cross-cultural interviews and implementation of other assessment practices to ensure cultural responsiveness; provide evidence or suggestions illustrating why certain behaviors are more reflective of learning differences rather than disabilities.

Type of Educator	Significant Multi-Tiered Team Contributions
General Class Teacher	Provide current and specific examples of needs of struggling learners; present documentation of attempted evidence-based interventions; share progress-monitoring results; provide insight into learner needs relative to the context of the total classroom environment; demonstrate evidence of culturally responsive education; share overall expertise of the content and process found in the Tier 1 core curriculum implemented.
Special Educator	Provide expertise in academic and emotional or behavioral needs of students with disabilities; assist in interpreting progress-monitoring data relative to observed behaviors; suggest accommodations needed to ensure appropriate assessment; assist in interpreting RTI results relative to exhibited classroom behaviors and learning needs; provide evidence that clarifies whether an intrinsic disorder exists if a disability is suspected; provide direct or indirect support for the implementation of interventions in all tiers of support; ensure proper referral procedures are followed if the learner is referred to special education.
Assessment Specialist	Provide accurate summary of results of progress monitoring and related assessment practices; provide clear evidence showing that the selected assessment devices and practices are culturally responsive and appropriate for intended uses with diverse learners; assist the learner's teachers with the implementation of culturally responsive assessment; ensure proper prerequisite intervention attempts are made and documented prior to a formal referral to special education.
Reading Specialist	Provide knowledge and expertise in the key areas in reading development including oral language, phonemic awareness, phonics, vocabulary, fluency, and comprehension; pinpoint specific reading strengths and weaknesses exhibited by the learner; help clarify appropriate reading objectives; present evidence-based reading interventions; identify necessary emergent and remedial reading skills support; assist with on-going progress monitoring and related assessment of reading growth.

Type of Educator	Significant Multi-Tiered Team Contributions
Speech/Language Specialist	Provide information about language needs and language disorders; clarify the differences between language needs related to the acquisition of English and a language disability due to problems intrinsic to the learner.
Parents/Guardians	Share cultural values/norms; discuss child's previous school experiences including successes and challenges; provide input into selected teaching strategies most appropriate for child based on cultural values/norms; discuss child's experiences in the community outside of the school environment; share family members' use of primary and/or second language in the home; provide insight into child's interactions with others outside of the school environment; express desires and aspirations for their child.
Paraprofessionals	Describe work completed with the student; share behaviors observed in one-to-one or small-group settings; provide insight into the academic and behavioral needs of the learner; assist in developing data-gathering procedures; share results of monitored and charted progress data gathered during work with the student.

At a minimum, problem-solving teams need expertise from each of these types of educators. Others may be involved (e.g., social worker or administrator) to support the team's efforts to make sound decisions about the cultural and linguistic needs of diverse learners. Form 8.1 provides a checklist for documenting contributions of various team members.

Essential Roles to Implement Tiered Instruction

Specific roles educators must assume, at any given time period in schools, are directly reflected in the trends and emphases associated with that timeframe. For example, since the 1970s efforts to provide increased education for students with disabilities in the general classroom (e.g., mainstreaming, inclusion) became more prevalent in schools nationwide. As a result, the roles of the special and general class teachers evolved and changed to reflect that emphasis in education, by requiring teachers to possess increased abilities to meet more diverse

of assessing and meeting social and behavioral needs along with academic needs in each of the Tiers. Similar to academic emphases in tiered learning, the implementation of social-emotional and behavior supports must reflect cultural and linguistic diversity if they are to be successful with all learners.

▶ **Culturally Responsive Skill Sets:** This role reflects the many abilities related to effective classroom management within the different tiers of instruction. Abilities to develop, implement, and evaluate effective classroom environments for successful education of all learners within multi-tiered instruction fall within this important role. A positive behavioral, supports-based emphasis on working with diverse learners who exhibit various social, emotional, and behavioral needs must be integrated throughout tiered instruction (Hoover & Patton, 2008). Also, as previously discussed, when educating diverse learners, behavior supports are often necessary to address behaviors associated with acculturative stress or stages of second language acquisition. This role assumes special relevance to diverse learners as educators strive to accurately interpret cultural and linguistic needs in a culturally responsive learning environment.

Collaborator

As emphasized throughout this chapter, educators must collaborate to meet the many diverse needs found in today's classrooms. In addition, collaboration among educators is often necessary and/or mandated to meet IDEA requirements for learners with special needs (Friend & Cook, 2003).

▶ **Culturally Responsive Skill Sets:** Culturally responsive collaboration includes those abilities needed to successfully interact with and support other educators to cooperatively implement instruction for diverse learners. Further, tiered instruction and RTI have made this role extremely important given the complex needs of diverse learners discussed throughout this book as well as the demands for cultural competence associated with referrals to special education.

Within these important roles various subskills exist, examples of which are provided in Figure 8.1. The figure, developed from information found in Hoover and Patton (2008), shows various subskills needed for the successful implementation of each of the five identified roles.

Problem-solving team members should evaluate their own abilities and training associated with each role and subskill to identify their strengths and if they require additional professional development to meet diverse learner needs in multi-tiered instruction and response to intervention. Form 8.2 (Guide to Self-Evaluating Multi-Tiered Roles), developed from Vaughn (2003), Yell (2004), Crone and Horner (2003), Hoover and Patton (2004, 2005a), Odom et al. (2005), Skrtic, Harris, and Shriner (2005), and Vaughn, Linan-Thompson, and Hickman (2003), provides a guide educators may use to evaluate their current abilities in selected subskills relative to each role.

In a recent research project conducted by the author, Form 8.2 was administered to over fifty educators who are beginning graduate training for state endorsements in both linguistically diverse and special education. Results show that as teachers with two to eight years' experience entering their graduate level training, they believe they possess average abilities in implementing these roles

FIGURE 8.1 Educator Roles and Associated Subskills in Multi-Tiered Instruction for Culturally and Linguistically Diverse Learners

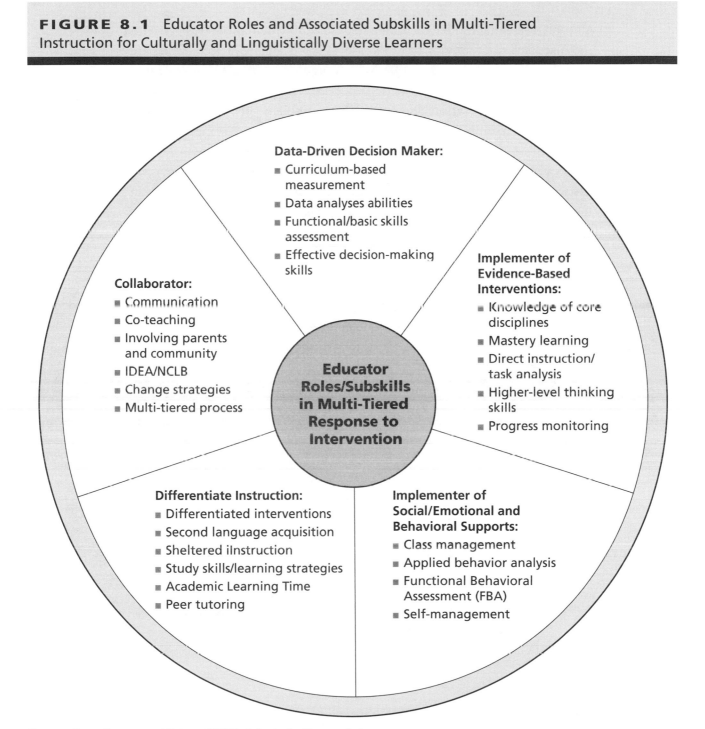

Source: From Hoover and Patton (2008). Adapted with permission.

with significant room for professional growth. Similarly, problem-solving team members may find results from this instrument helpful in guiding future professional development.

Collaboration within Tiered Instruction

A problem-solving model, including steps for implementation, was presented and discussed in Chapter 2, page 32. Also, as just discussed, selected roles are essential to effectively implement tiered learning along with problem-solving associated with RTI. In addition to the process and key multi-tiered instructional roles, several collaboration elements facilitate problem-solving team functioning and sustainability in today's schools. Walther-Thomas, Korinek, and McLaughlin (2005) identified six elements necessary for effective, sustainable collaboration. These are applicable to total school or district initiatives as well as to school-based problem-solving teams. The six elements are summarized in Table 8.1 and are followed by more in-depth discussions in the application of each of the elements to meet diverse needs within tiered instruction. The table was developed from discussions about these elements as found in Walther-

TABLE 8.1 Essential Elements for Effective Problem-Solving Team Collaboration

Element	Problem-Solving Team Implications
Shared Leadership	Everyone involved on the student's problem-solving team is included in the decision-making in meaningful ways either through direct contact or relevant representation
Coherent Vision	Refers to a collective vision shared among all team members concerning the direction to take to meet current and future needs
Comprehensive Planning	Refers to the careful consideration of all relevant factors related to implementing the vision
Adequate Resources	Includes the various materials, types of support, or personnel necessary to meet needs and complete team tasks
Sustained Implementation	This refers to the commitment to stay focused on tasks and processes needed to sustain the team efforts over the long term to ensure that what is implemented remains in place as new team members are included
Continuous Evaluation and Improvement	Effective collaboration includes on-going evaluation of its efforts with necessary modifications and adjustments made based on evaluative results to ensure long-term sustainability

Thomas et al. (2005). These six collaborative elements provide a solid structure for problem-solving teams to make effective data-driven decisions for diverse learners in their efforts to determine learning differences from disabilities.

Shared Leadership

Involving all team members in meaningful decision-making is the cornerstone to sharing leadership. In tiered instructional decision-making for diverse learners, implementation of this element is essential given the wide variety of skills needed to meet important cultural and linguistic needs. This includes the student, classroom, and home/community ecological factors summarized in Chapter 6. Simply stated, *there exists too much needed information and skills to adequately educate diverse learners in multi-tiered instruction to be entrusted to only one or two educators.* A team of educators, comprised of the individuals presented earlier in the chapter, must be in place so that diverse learners receive culturally responsive education and the team makes informed decisions as tiers or layers of instruction are implemented.

Coherent Vision

This element requires that problem-solving teams are committed to genuinely implementing culturally responsive tier instruction and RTI. It means that team members must be willing to increase their cultural competence/proficiency as discussed in Chapter 1 as well as modify and adapt the various assessment practices to reflect cultural and linguistic needs. This element also requires that problem-solving teams establish implementing culturally responsive education as their primary goal for educating diverse learners within tiered instruction. Additionally, this element allows educators to understand their individual contributions to the team. This, along with shared leadership, ensures that all team members' expertise is valued and used to make informed decisions necessary to differentiate learning differences from disabilities.

Comprehensive Planning

This collaborative element integrates tiered instructional goals, student characteristics, curricular benchmarks, available resources, as well as member roles and responsibilities to achieve the coherent team vision. This element also stresses the importance of assessing team strengths and areas of need resulting in the implementation of professional development to enhance team problem-solving abilities. In addition, according to Walther-Thomas, Korinek, and McLaughlin (2005), comprehensive planning involves identifying problem areas and gaps in services necessary to meet student needs. In regards to comprehensive planning for diverse learners educated within tiered instruction, the various student, classroom, and home/community ecological factors (refer to Table 6.1, page 109) must be addressed along with consideration of second language acquisition, cultural diversity and disability behaviors (refer to Table 1.2, page 16) to best prevent misinterpreting differences as disabilities. An overall goal of comprehensive planning for diverse learners is to engage all members of the problem-solving team to share their expertise to make the most informed culturally responsive decisions possible.

Adequate Resources

Without a doubt, if problem-solving teams lack adequate resources to complete their tasks, the education for all students suffers. The degree to which this significantly affects learner outcomes, effective decision-making, progress-monitoring/response-to-intervention results, and implementation of culturally responsive evidence-based interventions will vary based on the tiers or layers of intervention required as well as various cultural or linguistic factors (e.g., acculturation, stage of second language acquisition). Problem-solving teams require adequate support and resources especially given the diverse needs students bring to the classroom. The ability to effectively differentiate learning differences from learning or behavioral disorders is significantly limited if adequate resources are not made available to educators to meet cultural and linguistic needs. Teams must avoid considering struggling learner needs as disabilities until adequate resources are brought to the learning situation. In short, *lack of resources to successfully implement multi-tiered instruction and/or monitor response to interventions cannot be used as a reason for placing students into special education* in the hopes that additional resources might then be made available.

Sustained Implementation

Commitment to following through with support for the development of the five roles described is critical to maintaining long-term sustainability of tiered instruction, response to intervention, regular progress monitoring and data-driven decision-making. In regard to the education of diverse learners, cultural and linguistic factors may require more patience from educators in: (1) meeting expected benchmarks; (2) acquiring English as a second language; (3) acculturating to new learning environments; (4) processing information in English; or (5) learning accepted behaviors and norms in U.S. schools. As previously emphasized, ensuring that sufficient time, opportunity to learn, and resources exist must be facilitated by problem-solving teams if learning differences are to be accurately identified and not misinterpreted as learning or behavioral disorders.

Continuous Evaluation and Improvement

Problem-solving teams must be committed to evaluating their own performances and make necessary adjustments if warranted. If teams stay true to considering the ecological factors of student, classroom, and home/community, most cultural and linguistic needs of diverse learners will be incorporated into multi-tiered instruction. Similarly, if the progress-monitoring activities and related assessment practices are culturally responsive, teams will be able to feel highly confident in their abilities to make informed decisions. Therefore, problem-solving teams must self-evaluate in open and honest ways to sustain their work and support for all team members, as well as assist diverse learners to successfully meet curricular benchmarks over the long term.

SUMMARY

While tiered instruction/RTI may help to facilitate more effective opportunities to learn, the lack of adequate progress should not be considered a "student problem" until the six collaboration elements have been implemented in good faith by problem-solving teams. In addition, given the fact that some learners may be eventually referred for special education due to insufficient progress toward benchmarks through a multi-tiered/RTI system, it is critical to avoid erroneously removing a diverse learner from Tier 1 and educating that student in Tiers 2 or 3 until sufficient collaboration efforts among team members has occurred. As emphasized throughout this chapter, effective collaboration and mastery of the contemporary roles identified as necessary to implement tiered instruction, serve to assist problem-solving teams to more consistently avoid misinterpreting lack of progress from lack of opportunity. This, in turn, provides problem-solving teams a greater ability to differentiate learning differences from learning or behavior disabilities.

Additional Activities to Support Learner Outcomes

1. Evaluate your school's problem-solving team to determine if all needed members to meet diverse needs are contributing members (Form 8.1).

2. Complete the self-evaluation guide (Form 8.2) on your knowledge and skills associated with the five roles. Develop a professional plan to increase your abilities in areas needing further development.

3. Evaluate the resources necessary to meet the needs of diverse learners in your school and the extent to which they are available to the problem-solving team.

4. Develop a comprehensive plan for implementing the six collaboration elements in your school's problem-solving team process.

Student _____ Date _____

Instructions: Check each item relative to the decision-making process when made by problem-solving team members.

ESL/Bilingual Educator's Contributions

_____ Cultural and linguistic issues pertaining to the suspected area of need

_____ Assist to put response to intervention results in cultural/linguistic context

_____ Clarify learning needs associated with acculturation

_____ Clarify learning needs associated with acquisition of a second language

_____ Assist in completing cross-cultural interviews

_____ Assist with the selection and use of culturally responsive assessment practices

_____ Help to accurately interpret assessment results within a culturally responsive context

_____ Provide insight/evidence as to why suspected learning problems are more reflective of learning differences

_____ Suggest accommodations to ensure opportunities to learn to meet cultural/linguistic needs

General Class Teacher's Contributions

_____ Provide documented evidence of student's learning needs

_____ Present documentation of results of evidence-based interventions used in the classroom

_____ Provide examples of culturally responsive education relative to student's suspected learning problems

_____ Share expertise of the content and process found within Tier 1 instruction

_____ Share documented progress-monitoring results

Special Educator's Contributions

_____ Provide expertise in academic and social-emotional needs of students with learning or behavior disorders

_____ Assist in the interpretation of progress-monitoring data relative to observable classroom behaviors

_____ Suggest accommodations to ensure appropriate opportunities to learn to meet suspected disability needs

_____ Provide evidence to clarify whether an intrinsic disorder exists

_____ Provide direct and/or indirect support to general educators in each Tier of instruction

_____ Ensure that proper prereferral and referral procedures are followed if learner is referred for special education assessment and possible placement

Assessment Specialist's Contributions

_____ Provide accurate summaries of assessment results

_____ Provide clear evidence demonstrating that the selected assessment devices and practices are culturally responsive

_____ Assist the learner's teachers with culturally responsive assessment

_____ Ensure that proper prerequisite interventions are attempted and results documented prior to formal referral to special education

Reading Specialist's Contributions

_____ Provide knowledge/expertise in key reading development areas

_____ Assist in pinpointing student's specific reading strengths/weaknesses

_____ Clarify reading objectives and desired outcomes based on needs

_____ Select/discuss appropriate evidence-based reading interventions

_____ Assist with on-going progress monitoring and reporting of results in reading

_____ Interpret formal and informal reading assessment results

Speech/Language Specialist's Contributions

_____ Provide information about language needs and language disorders

_____ Clarify the differences between a language difference and a language disorder

_____ Provide speech/language support to general class teachers in each Tier of instruction

_____ Identify evidence-based speech/language interventions for use in each Tier of intervention

Parents'/Guardians' Contributions

_____ Share cultural values and norms

_____ Share prior school experiences

_____ Discuss child's community experiences

_____ Determine primary language spoken in the home

_____ Express their desires/aspirations for their child

_____ Discuss child's interactions with peers outside of school, including language most used

Paraprofessional's Contributions

_____ Describe work completed with learner

_____ Share and discuss behaviors observed while working with student

_____ Share ideas on student's needs

_____ Assist in gathering progress-monitoring data

_____ Share results of gathered progress-monitoring data

Instructions: Rate your level of preparation for each item:

1 = None

2 = Little (e.g., Completed a workshop)

3 = Some (e.g., Some coverage in a few courses/workshops)

4 = Extensive (e.g., Emphasized in several courses/workshops)

5 = Highly Extensive (e.g., Focus area in college training)

Data-Driven Decision-Making	None		Some		Highly Extensive
Curriculum-based measurement	1	2	3	4	5
Strategies for effective decision-making	1	2	3	4	5
Data analysis	1	2	3	4	5
Multiple monitoring strategies	1	2	3	4	5
Basic skills assessment	1	2	3	4	5
Functional skills assessment	1	2	3	4	5
Special education eligibility process/criteria	1	2	3	4	5

Evidence-Based Intervention					
Knowledge of core disciplines	1	2	3	4	5
Higher-order thinking skills	1	2	3	4	5
Evidence-based instructional strategies	1	2	3	4	5
Task analysis	1	2	3	4	5
Direct instruction	1	2	3	4	5
Programmed instruction	1	2	3	4	5
Impact of culture and language on learning	1	2	3	4	5
Determining difference versus disability	1	2	3	4	5
Compensatory strategies for specific disabilities	1	2	3	4	5
Functional living and transition skills	1	2	3	4	5
Mastery learning	1	2	3	4	5

Socioemotional and Behavioral Supports					
Classroom management	1	2	3	4	5
Behavior management	1	2	3	4	5
Applied behavioral analysis	1	2	3	4	5
Targeted behavioral supports	1	2	3	4	5
Social skills instruction	1	2	3	4	5
Self-management skills instruction	1	2	3	4	5
Impact of culture and language on behavior	1	2	3	4	5
Social-emotional development	1	2	3	4	5
Functional Behavioral Assessment	1	2	3	4	5
Positive Behavioral supports/behavioral plans	1	2	3	4	5

Differentiation	None		Some		Highly Extensive
Accommodations and modifications	1	2	3	4	5
Differentiation strategies	1	2	3	4	5
Second language acquisition	1	2	3	4	5
Culturally relevant instruction	1	2	3	4	5
Sheltered instruction	1	2	3	4	5
Study skills and learning strategies	1	2	3	4	5
Student peer tutoring models	1	2	3	4	5
Targeted ALT (time, task focus, intensity)	1	2	3	4	5
Scheduling strategies	1	2	3	4	5
Alternative curriculum and materials	1	2	3	4	5
Adapting to address functional living abilities	1	2	3	4	5

Collaboration					
Communication skills	1	2	3	4	5
Co-teaching/team processes	1	2	3	4	5
Consulting/coaching	1	2	3	4	5
Change strategies	1	2	3	4	5
Parent-school-community partnerships	1	2	3	4	5
Cultural/linguistic diversity and collaboration	1	2	3	4	5
Working with parents on IEP and disability-related issues	1	2	3	4	5
Knowledge/understanding of IDEA	1	2	3	4	5
Knowledge of district SPED procedures	1	2	3	4	5
Knowledge of school/district RTI	1	2	3	4	5

Summarize areas requiring additional professional development:

Source: From Hoover and Patton (2008). Adapted with permission.

Differentiated Support Interventions

As discussed, the need to differentiate instruction is an integral part of effectively implementing multi-tiered instruction. As evidence-based interventions are implemented for diverse learners, cultural and linguistic diverse needs require teachers to make specific adjustments in the classroom within the broad context of evidence-based interventions. Numerous *support interventions* exist to add value to evidence-based interventions to best meet diverse needs requiring instructional differentiations.

Table A.1 describes numerous interventions that teachers may find valuable to support tiered instruction as individual diverse needs indicate. Specific considerations for implementing each with diverse learners are also provided. This appendix was developed from content found in a variety of sources including Polloway, Patton, and Serna (2008), Baca and Cervantes (2004), and Hoover and Patton (2005a).

Intervention	Process	Desired Outcomes	Diverse Considerations
Learning Center	Creating a designated area where instructional materials are available for use by individual or small groups of students	Students reinforce learning at their own pace	Center should contain visual or auditory stimuli reflective of cultural backgrounds
Alternative Method for Response	Adapting mode of response for learners	Students respond to learning in a manner consistent with their needs	Cultural values may support response modes that vary from others in the classroom and these should be respected by teachers
Shortened Assignments	Breaking down longer assignments into shorter, more manageable tasks	Difficult or complex tasks are more easily completed by students	Students in the process of acquiring a second language and/or acculturating to a new environment may initially respond more easily to shorter assignments
Role Playing	Students assume roles and act these out based on their perceptions of the roles	Students acquire a greater understanding of acceptable behaviors in different types of situations	Understanding diverse values and customs occurs through role playing; acculturative stress may be more easily managed through role playing
Providing Choices	Students can select tasks or assignments to complete or the order in which they complete assigned tasks	Students manage time and organize their completion of assignments; reduces anxiety with assignment completion	Allows learners to manage time and organize themselves based on cultural values and preferred instructional styles
Contingency Contracting	An agreement between teacher and student concerning academics or behaviors	Improve motivation; support preferred ways of learning; assume greater ownership in learning	Cultural values may be incorporated into contracts; second language acquisition needs can be accommodated through contracts

Intervention	Process	Desired Outcomes	Diverse Considerations
Modify Presentation of Abstract Concepts	Scaffolding; use of concrete procedures to assist learners with abstract concepts	Abstract concepts are made more comprehensible to learners based on linguistic abilities	As second language learners begin to develop academic language skills (CALP) this intervention assists in building on students' prior experiences to increase success
Prompting	Providing cues and supports to facilitate learning and response	Support learning to encourage and maintain interest and success	Prompting must reflect cultural values or teachings to be most effective
Simplify Reading Levels	Reducing and minimizing the complexities of language and vocabulary in printed material	Provide learners with language and vocabulary commensurate with their English language development	Both L1 and L2 vocabulary should be included to ensure success as students acquire a second language and/or acculturate to a new learning environment
Signal Interference	Using nonverbal cues or signals to manage behavior or support student actions	Prevent minor behaviors from becoming more significant without drawing attention away from the classroom instruction; provide a positive gesture to support learner actions within the context of the instruction	Signals must be culturally meaningful to be effective and be viewed as positive gestures to avoid misrepresenting actions as counter to cultural norms
Proximity Control	Strategic positioning of the student to provide emotional support and/or minimize potential for behavior problems	Increase confidence in own abilities as well as time on task behaviors	Use of personal space or proximity may vary significantly across cultures and must be considered
Planned Ignoring	Purposefully ignoring select minor behaviors	Reduce negative behaviors by not drawing attention to or reinforcing them	Second language acquisition behaviors may indicate lack of understanding and should not be ignored
Clearly Articulated Expectations	Providing students with a clear set of directions and steps for learning	Minimize frustration or anxiety due to unfamiliar or confusing academic and behavioral expectations	Second language learners and/or those acculturating to a new environment often require explicit directions and instruction to best meet their cultural and linguistic needs
Planned Physical Movement	Providing students planned opportunities to actively engage in learning activities through movement within the classroom	Generate active participation in learning and reduce behavior problems associated with extensive passive activities	This intervention supports diverse learners' needs for active learning and on-going verbal dialogue to facilitate the development of a second language
Student Accountability	Providing structures that allow students to be accountable for their actions and learning	Students become more aware of their actions and impact on own learning and behaviors	Different cultures may view individual accountability in various ways; group accountability might be preferred over individual achievements and this must be reflected in accountability practices in the classroom
Self-Monitoring	Students monitor and evaluate their own learning and behaviors	Encourage positive learning; increase time on task; minimize behavior problems	Effective intervention for helping students acculturate to a new learning environment

RTI, Evidence-Based, Curriculum-Based, Special Education, and Diversity Education Websites

A variety of websites exist that provide resources on the topics of response to intervention, evidence-based interventions, progress-monitoring, special education, and the education of culturally and linguistically diverse learners. These sites were selected and located through an author review of available websites that address topics, services, and/or training that relate to issues important to discerning learning differences from disabilities.

Site	Target Area(s)	Site Address*
Center for Data-Driven Reform	Data-Driven Reform	www.cddre.org/Mission.cfm
University of Minnesota, College of Education and Human Development	Curriculum-Based Measurement	http://cehd.umn.edu/EdPsych/SpecialEd/CBMConference/handouts.html
National Association of State Directors of Special Education	Educational Outcomes	www.nasdse.org/about.cfm
The National Center for Culturally Responsive Educational Systems (NCCRESt)	Culturally Responsive Education	www.nccrest.org/index.html
AIMSweb®	Formative Assessment	www.aimsweb.com
Coalition for Evidence-Based Policy	Evidence-based Education	www.evidencebasedprograms.org/Default.aspx?tabid=138
Curriculum-Based Measurement Warehouse	Curriculum-based Measurement	www.interventioncentral.org/htmdocs/interventions/cbmwarehouse.php
Dynamic Indicators of Basic Early Literacy Skills (DIBELS)	Reading Fluency	http://dibels.uoregon.edu/index.php
Iris Center	Special Education	http://iris.peabody.vanderbilt.edu/index.html
National Research Center on Learning Disabilities (NRCLD)	Learning Disabilities	www.nrcld.org/
National Reading Panel	Reading	www.nationalreadingpanel.org/default.htm

* Each website in this appendix was a working site at time of publication; however, status of sites may have changed over time.

Site	Target Area(s)	Site Address*
Promising Practices Network (PPN)	Evidence-Based	www.promisingpractices.net/
Positive Behavioral Interventions and Supports-OSEP	PBS	www.pbis.org/main.htm
Research Institute on Progress Monitoring	CBM	www.progressmonitoring.net/ RIPMProducts2.html
RTI Partnership at UCR	RTI	www.rti.ucr.edu/rtimaterials.htm
Success for All Foundation	Learners At-Risk	www.successforall.net/about/
The Access Center	Special Education	www.k8accesscenter.org/index.php
Vaughn Gross Center for Reading and Language Arts (VGC)	Reading	www.texasreading.org/utcrla/
Center for Research on Learning-KU	Strategy Interventions	www.kucrl.org/about/press.shtml
What Works Clearinghouse	Evidence-Based	http://ies.ed.gov/ncee/wwc/
International Reading Association	RTI	www.reading.org/resources/issues/ focus_rti.html

References

Abedi, J. (2004). *Psychometric issues in ELL assessment and special education eligibility*. Paper presented at the "English Language Learners Struggling to Learn: Emergent Research on Linguistic Differences and Learning Disabilities Conference." Tempe, AZ.

Allen, R. V. (1976). *Language experiences in communication*. Boston: Houghton Mifflin.

Allinder, R. M., Fuchs, L. S., & Fuchs, D. (2004). Issues in curriculum-based assessment. In A. M. Sorrells, H. Reith, & P. Sindelar (eds.), *Critical issues in special education: Access, diversity and accountability* (pp. 106–124). Boston: Allyn & Bacon.

Allsopp, D. H. (1997). Using classwide peer tutoring to teach beginning algebra problem-solving skills in heterogeneous classrooms. *Remedial and Special Education, 18*, 367–379.

Arreaga-Mayer, C. (1998). Increasing active student responding and improving academic performance through classwide peer tutoring. *Intervention in School and Clinic, 34*, 89–94.

Artiles, A. J., Trent, S. C., & Palmer, J. (2004). Culturally diverse students in special education: Legacies and prospects. In J. A. Banks & C. M. Banks (eds.), *Handbook of research on multicultural education* (2nd ed., pp. 716–735). San Francisco, CA: Jossey-Bass.

Atwell, N. (1998). *In the middle: New understanding about writing, reading, and learning*. Portsmouth, NH: Heinemann.

Baca, L. M. (2005). The education of English language learners with special needs. In J. J. Hoover (ed.), *Current issues in special education* (pp. 25–33). Boulder: University of Colorado, Boulder.

Baca, L., & Cervantes, H. T. (2004). *The bilingual special education interface*. Columbus: Merrill.

Baca, L. M., & Clark, C. (November 1992). *EXITO: A dynamic team assessment approach for culturally diverse students*. Minneapolis, MN. Paper presented at CEC Topical Conference.

Banks, J. A. (1994). *Multiethnic education: Theory and practice*. Boston: Allyn & Bacon.

Bender, W. N. (2002). *Differentiating instruction for students with learning disabilities: Best teaching practices for general and special educators*. Thousand Oaks, CA: Corwin.

Bender, W. N., & Shores, C. (2007). *Response to intervention: A practical guide for every teacher*. Thousand Oaks, CA: Corwin.

Biglan, A., Mrazek, P. J., Carnine, D., & Flay, B. R. (2003). The integration of research and practice in the prevention of youth problem behaviors. *American Psychologist, 58*, 433–441.

Bradley, R., Danielson, L., & Hallahan, D. P. (2002). *Identification of learning disabilities: Research to practice*. Mahwah, NJ: Erlbaum.

Brown-Chidsey, R., & Steege, M. W. (2005). *Response to intervention: Principles and strategies for effective practice*. New York: Guilford Press.

Bronfenbrenner, U. (1979). *The ecology of human development*. Cambridge, MA: Harvard University Press.

Bronfenbrenner, U. (1995). Developmental ecology through space and time: A future perspective. In P. Moen, G. Elder, and K. Leuscher (eds.), *Examining lives in context: Perspectives on the ecology of human development* (pp. 619–647). Washington, DC: American Psychological Association.

Brown, L. (2004). Evaluating and managing classroom behavior. In D. D. Hammill and N. R. Bartel (eds.), *Teaching students with learning and behavior problems* (pp. 255–290). Austin, TX: Pro-Ed.

Carroll, J. B. (1963). A model of school learning. *Teachers College Record, 64*, 723–733.

Chalfant, J. C., Pysh, M. V. D., & Moultrie, R. (1979). Teacher assistance teams—A model for within-building problem solving. *Learning Disability Quarterly, 2*(3), 85–96.

Chamot, A. U., & O'Malley, J. M. (1996). The cognitive academic language learning approach (CALLA): A model for linguistically diverse classrooms. *Elementary School Journal, 96*(3), 259–273.

Clay, M. (1993). *Reading recovery: A guidebook for teachers in training*. Portsmouth, NH: Heinemann.

Clay, M. (1985). *The early detection of reading difficulties* (3rd ed.). Portsmouth, NH: Heinemann.

Cohen, L. G., Spenciner, L. J., & Twitchell, D. E. (2003). Assessment of social-emotional development in young children. In M. J. Breen and C. R. Fiedler (eds.), *Behavioral approach to assessment of youth with emotional/behavioral disorders: A handbook for school-based practitioners* (pp. 497–558). Austin, TX: Pro-Ed.

Collier, V. P., & Thomas, W. P. (1989). How quickly can immigrants become proficient in English? *Journal of Educational Issues of Language Minority Students, 5*, 25–38.

Coyne, M. D., Kame'enui, E. J., & Carnine, D. N. (2007). *Effective teaching strategies that accommodate diverse learners*. Columbus, OH: Pearson.

Crone, D. A., & Horner, R. H. (2003). *Building positive behavior support systems in schools: Functional behavioral assessment*. New York: Guilford Press.

Cross, T., Brazron, B., Dennis, K., & Isaacs, M. (1989). *Towards a culturally competent system of care*. Washington, DC: CASSP Technical Assistance Center, Georgetown University Child Development Center.

Cummins, J. (2000). *Language, power, and pedagogy: Bilingual children in the crossfire*. Clevedon, England: Multilingual Matters Limited.

Cummins, J. (1989). A theoretical framework for bilingual and special education. *Exceptional Children, 56*(2), 111–119.

Damico, J. S., Cheng, J., Deleon, J., Ferrer, J., & Westernoff, F. (November 1992). *Descriptive assessment in the schools: Meeting new challenges with new solutions*. Minneapolis, MN. Paper presented at CEC Topical Conference.

De La Colina, M. G., Parker, R. I., Hasbrouck, J. E., & Lara-Alecio, R. (2001). Intensive intervention in reading fluency for at-risk beginning Spanish readers. *Bilingual Research Journal, 25,* 503–538.

de Valenzuela, J. S., & Baca, L. M. (2004). Procedures and techniques for assessing the bilingual exceptional child. In L. M. Baca and H. Cervantes (eds.), *The bilingual special education interface* (pp. 187–201). Columbus: Merrill.

Deno, S. L. (2005). Problem-solving assessment. In R. Brown-Chidsey (ed.), *Assessment for intervention: A problem-solving approach* (pp. 10–40). New York: Guilford.

Deno, S. L., & Fuchs, L. S. (1987). Developing curriculum-based measurement systems for data-based special education problem-solving. *Focus on Exceptional Children, 19,* 1–16.

Denton, C. A., Anthony, J. L., Parker, R., & Hasbrouck, J. (2004). Effects of two tutoring programs on the English reading development of Spanish-English bilingual students. *The Elementary School Journal, 104,* 289–305.

Donovan, M. S., & Cross, C. T. (2002). *Minority students in special education and gifted education.* Washington, DC: National Academy Press.

Durand, V. M., & Carr, E. G. (1985). Self-injurious behavior: Motivating conditions and guidelines for treatment. *School Psychology Review, 14*(2), 171–176.

Education Week. (2003). *Quality Counts 2003: If I can't learn from you.* www.edweek.org. Retrieved May 1, 2007. Author.

Eisner, E. W. (2001). *The educational imagination: On design and evaluation of school programs* (3rd ed.). Upper Saddle River, NJ: Prentice Hall.

Elliot, S. N., Braden, J. P., & White, J. L. (2001). *Assessing one and all: Educational accountability for students with disabilities.* Arlington, VA: Council for Exceptional Children.

Engelmann, S., & Carnine, D. (1982). *Theory of instruction: Principles and applications.* New York: Irvington.

Farr, B., & Turnbull, E. (1997). *Assessment alternatives for diverse classrooms.* Norwood, MA: Christopher-Gordon.

Fiedler, C. R. (2003). Legal and ethical issues in the educational assessment for youth with emotional/behavioral disorders. In M. J. Breen and C. R. Fiedler (eds.), *Behavioral approach to assessment of youth with emotional/behavioral disorders: A handbook for school-based practitioners* (pp. 21–72). Austin, TX: Pro-Ed.

Figueroa, R. A., & Newsome, P. (2004). The diagnosis of learning disabilities in English language learners—Is it nondiscriminatory? Paper presented at the 2004 NCCRESt Conference, *English Language Learners Struggling to Learn: Emergent Research on Linguistic Differences and Learning Disabilities,* Tempe, AZ.

Flood, J., & Lapp, D. (1988). A reader response approach to the teaching of literature. *Reading Research and Instruction, 27,* 61–66.

Friend, M. & Cook, L. (2003). *Interactions: Collaboration skills for school professionals* (4th ed.). Boston: Allyn & Bacon.

Fuchs, L. S. (2003). Assessing intervention responsiveness: Conceptual and technical issues. *Learning Disabilities Research and Practice, 18*(3), 172–186.

Fuchs, D., & Fuchs, L. S. (2006). Introduction to response to intervention: What, why, and how valid is it? *Reading Research Quarterly, 41*(1), 93–99.

Fuchs, D., Mock, D., Morgan, P. L., & Young, C. (2003). Responsiveness to intervention: Definitions, evidence, and implications for the learning disabilities construct. *Learning Disabilities: Research & Practice, 18*(3), 157–171.

Fung, I Y. Y., Wilkinson, I. A. G., & Moore, D. W. (2003). L1–assisted reciprocal teaching to improve ESL students' comprehension of English expository text. *Learning and Instruction, 13,* 1–13.

Galland, P. A. (1995). An evaluation of the Cognitive Academic Language Learning Approach (CALLA) in the High Intensity Language Training (HILT) Science Program in Arlington Public Schools. Unpublished Master's research paper, Georgetown University.

Garcia, G., & Pearson, P. (1994). Assessment and diversity. In L. Darling-Hammond (ed.), *A Review of Research in Education* (pp. 337–391). Washington, DC: American Educational Research Association.

Good, T. L., & Brophy, J. E. (1995). *Contemporary educational psychology.* New York: Longman.

Gough, D. (2004). Systemic research synthesis. In G. Thomas and R. Pring (eds.), *Evidence-based practice in education* (pp. 44–62). New York: Open University Press.

Greenwood, C. R., Arreaga-Mayer, C., Utley, C. A., Gavin, K. M., & Terry, B. J. (2001). Classwide peer tutoring learning management system: Applications with elementary-level English language learners. *Remedial and Special Education, 22,* 34–47.

Grossman, H. (1995). *Special education in a diverse society.* Boston: Allyn & Bacon.

Haager, D., Klingner, J., & Vaughn, S. (2007). *Evidence-based reading practices for response to intervention.* Baltimore, MD: Brookes Publishing.

Haager, D., & Klingner, J. K. (2005). *Differentiating instruction in inclusive classrooms: The special educator's guide.* Boston: Pearson.

Hallahan, D. P., Lloyd, J. W., Kauffman, J. M., Weiss, M. P., & Martinez, E. A. (2005). *Learning disabilities: Foundations, characteristics, and effective teaching.* Boston: Pearson.

Hamayan, E. V., & Damico, J. S. (1991). Developing and using a second language. In E. V. Hamayan and J. S. Damico (eds.), *Limiting bias in the assessment of bilingual students* (pp. 39–75). Austin, TX: Pro-Ed.

Hammill, D. D. (1987). An overview of assessment practices. In D. D. Hammill (ed.), *Assessing the abilities and instructional needs of students* (pp. 1–15). Austin, TX: Pro-Ed.

Hammill, D. D., & Bartel, N. R. (2004). *Teaching students with learning and behavior problems.* Austin, TX: Pro-Ed.

Hancock, M. R. (1993). Exploring and extending personal response through literature response journals. *The Reading Teacher, 46,* 466–474.

Hanley, J. (1999). Beyond the tip of the iceberg: Five stages toward cultural competence. *Today's Youth: The Community Circle of Caring Journal, 3*(2), 9–12.

Herman, J. L., Aschbacher, P. R., & Winters. L. (1992). *A practical guide to alternative assessment.* Alexandria, VA: Association for Supervision and Curriculum Development.

Hodgkinson, H. (2000). *Educational demographics: What teachers should know.* Alexandria, VA: Association for Supervision and Curriculum Development.

Hoover, J. J., & Méndez Barletta, L. M. (2008). Considerations when assessing ELLs for special education. In J. K. Klingner, J. J. Hoover, and L. Baca (eds.), *English language learners who struggle with reading: Language acquisition or learning disabilities?* (pp. 93–108). Thousand Oaks, CA: Corwin.

Hoover, J. J. (2008). Data-driven decision-making in a multi-tiered model. In J. K. Klingner, J. J. Hoover, and L. Baca (eds.), *English language learners who struggle with reading: Language acquisition or learning disabilities?* (pp. 75–92). Thousand Oaks, CA: Corwin.

Hoover, J. J. (2006). *Framework for implementing culturally competent response to intervention* (Invited Presentation). Summit on Differentiated Instruction and Academic Intervention. New York: NYC Public Schools, April 25, 2006.

Hoover, J. J. (2005). Special challenges, special needs. In J. J. Hoover (ed.), *Current issues in special education: Meeting diverse needs in the twenty-first century* (pp. 1–3). Boulder, CO: University of Colorado, School of Education, BUENO Center.

Hoover, J. J. (2001). *Assessment of English language learners* (CD-ROM). Boulder, CO: University of Colorado at Boulder, BUENO Center.

Hoover, J. J. (1991). *Classroom applications of cognitive learning styles.* Boulder, CO: Hamilton Publications.

Hoover, J. J., Klingner, J., Baca, L. M., & Patton, J. M. (2008). *Methods for teaching culturally and linguistically diverse exceptional learners.* Columbus, OH: Pearson.

Hoover, J. J., & Patton, J. R. (2008). Role of special educators in multi-tiered instructional programming. *Intervention in School and Clinic, 43,* 195–202.

Hoover, J. J., & Patton, J. R. (2005a). *Curriculum adaptations for students with learning and behavior problems: Differentiating instruction to meet diverse needs* (3rd ed.). Austin, TX: Pro-Ed.

Hoover, J. J., & Patton, J. R. (2005b). Differentiating curriculum and instruction for English language learners with special needs. *Intervention in School and Clinic, 40,* 231–235.

Hoover, J. J., & Patton, J. R. (2004). Perspective: Differentiating standards-based education for students with diverse needs. *Remedial and Special Education, 25*(2), 74–78.

Hoover, J. J., & Collier, C. (2004). Methods and materials for bilingual special education. In L. M. Baca & H. Cervantes, *The bilingual special education interface,* pp. 274–297. Columbus: Merrill.

Hoover, J. J., & Collier, C. (2003). *Learning styles* (CD-ROM). Boulder, CO: University of Colorado at Boulder BUENO Center.

Hoover, J. J., & Collier, C. (1985). Referring culturally different children: Sociocultural considerations. *Academic Therapy, 20*(4), 503–509.

Hoover, J. J., Patton, J. R., Hresko, W., & Hammill, D. (in development). *Basic skills rating system.* Austin, TX: Pro-Ed.

Horner, R. H. (2000). Positive behavior supports. In M. L. Wehmeyer and J. R. Patton (eds.), *Mental retardation in the 21st century* (pp. 181–196). Austin, TX: Pro-Ed.

Hosp, J. L., & Reschly, D. J. (2004). Disproportionate representation of minority students in special education: Academic, demographic, and economic predictors. *Exceptional Children, 70*(2), 185–199.

Hosp, M. K., Hosp, J. L., & Howell, K. W. (2007). *The ABC's of CBM: A practical guide to curriculum-based measurement.* New York: The Guilford Press.

IDEA. (2004). *Individuals with Disabilities Education Act Amendments of 2004,* Washington, DC. Senate Bill 1248.

Idol, L., Nevin, A., & Paolucci-Whitcomb, P. (1995). The collaborative consultation model. *Journal of Educational and Psychological Consultation, 6*(4), 347–361.

Jimerson, S. R., Burns, M. K., & VanDerHeyden, A. M. (eds.). (2007). *Response to intervention: The science and practice of assessment an intervention.* New York: Springer.

Johnson, D. W., & Johnson, R. T. (1993). Forward. In J. W. Putnam (ed.), *Cooperative learning and strategies for inclusion* (pp. xii–xiv). Baltimore, MD: Brookes Publishing.

Kagan, S., & High, J. (2002). Kagan structures for English language learners. *ESL Magazine, 5*(4), 10–12.

Kampwirth, T. J. (2006). *Collaborative consultation in the schools: Effective practice for students with learning and behavior problems.* Columbus, OH: Pearson.

Keller, F. S. (1968). Goodbye teacher . . . *Journal of Applied Behavior Analysis, 1,* 79–89.

Klingner, J. K., Artiles, A. J., & Méndez Barletta, L. M. (2004). English language learners who struggle with reading: Language acquisition or learning disabilities? Paper presented at the Research Conference *English Language Learners Struggling to Learn: Emergent Research on Linguistic Differences and Learning Disabilities,* Scottsdale, AZ, November.

Klingner, J. K., & Bianco, M. (2006). What is special about special education for culturally and linguistically diverse students with disabilities? In B. Cook & B. Schirmer (eds.), *What is special about special education?* (pp. 37–53). Austin, TX: PRO-ED.

Klingner, J. K., Méndez Barletta, L. M., & Hoover, J. J. (2008). Response to Intervention Models and English language learners. In J. K. Klingner, J. J. Hoover, and L. Baca (eds.), *English language learners who struggle with reading: Language acquisition or learning disabilities?* (pp. 37–50). Thousand Oaks, CA: Corwin.

Klingner, J. K., & Edwards, P. E. (2006). Cultural considerations with response to intervention models. *Reading Research Quarterly 41*(1), 108–115.

Klingner, J., Sorrells, A. M., & Barrera, M. T. (2007). Considerations when implementing response to intervention with culturally and linguistically diverse students. In D. Hagger, J. Klingner, & S. Vaughn (eds.), *Evidence-based reading practices for response to intervention* (pp. 223–244). Baltimore, MD: Paul H. Brookes.

Klingner, J. K., Vaughn, S., Dimino, J., Schumm, J. S., & Bryant, D. P. (2001). *From clunk to click: Collaborative strategic reading.* Longmont, CO: Sopris West.

Klingner, J. K., & Vaughn, S. (2000). The helping behaviors of fifth-graders while using collaborative strategic reading (CSR) during ESL content classes. *TESOL Quarterly, 34,* 69–98.

Klingner, J. K., & Vaughn, S. (1996). Reciprocal teaching of reading comprehension strategies for students with learning disabilities who use English as a second language. *Elementary School Journal, 96,* 275–293.

Krashen, S. D., Long, M., & Scarcella, R. (1979). Age, rate and eventual attainment in second language acquisition. *TESOL Quarterly, 13*, 573–582.

Lachat, M. A. (2004). *Standards-based instruction and assessment for English language learners.* Thousand Oaks, CA: Corwin.

Marston, D., Reschly, A. L., Lau, M. Y., Muyskens, P., & Canter, A. (2007). Historical perspectives and current trends in problem solving: The Minnesota story. In D. Hagger, J. Klingner, & S. Vaughn (eds.), *Evidence-based reading practices for response to intervention* (pp. 265–285). Baltimore, MD: Paul H. Brookes.

Mason, J. L. (1993). *Cultural Competence Self-Assessment Questionnaire.* Portland, OR: Portland State University. Multicultural Initiative Project.

McCook, J. E. (2006). *The RTI guide: Developing and implementing a model in your schools.* Horsham, PA: LRP Publications.

McLaughlin, B. (1985). *Second-language acquisition in childhood* (vol. 2). Hillsdale, NJ: Lawrence Erlbaum.

McLaughlin, W. W., & Shepard, L. A. (1995). *Improving education through standards-based reform.* Stanford, CA: The National Academy of Education.

McMillan, J. H. (2001). *Essential assessment concepts for teachers and administrators.* Thousand Oaks, CA: Corwin Press.

Meese, R. L. (2001). *Teaching learners with mild disabilities: Integrating research with practice* (2nd ed.). Belmont, CA: Wadsworth/Thomson Learning.

Moran, D. J., & Malott, R. W. (2004). *Evidenced-based educational methods.* Boston: Elsevier Academic Press.

National Research Council. (2002). *Scientific research in education.* Washington, DC: National Academies Press.

NRCLD (2005). Responsiveness to Intervention in the SLD Determination Process. National Research Center on Learning Disabilities (NRCLD). Author. www.nrcld.org. Online. Accessed: May 28, 2007.

National Reading Panel. (2000). *Teaching children to read: An evidence-based assessment of the scientific research literature on reading and its implications for reading instruction: summary report.* Washington, DC: National Institute of Child Health and Development.

Nazarro, J. N. (1981). *Culturally diverse exceptional children.* Reston, VA: Council for Exceptional Children.

Neal, J. C., & Kelly, P. R. (1999). The success of Reading Recovery for English language learners and *Descubriendo La Lectura* for bilingual students in California. *Literacy Teaching and Learning, 2*, 81–108.

Nieto, S. (1996). *Affirming diversity* (2nd ed.). New York: Longman.

NJCLD-National Joint Committee on Learning Disabilities (2005). *Responsiveness to intervention and learning disabilities.* Author. Retrieved online 5/1/07 from www.ldonline.org/NJCLD.

No Child Left Behind Act; The Elementary and Secondary Education Act of 2001, P.L. 107-110, 115, *Stat.1425* (2001). Washington, DC.

Odom, S. L., Brantlinger, E., Gersten, R., Horner, R. H., Thompson, B., & Karris, K. R. (2005). Research in special education: Scientific methods and evidence-based practices. *Exceptional Children, 71*(2), 137–148.

O'Malley, J. M. (1988). The cognitive academic language learning approach (CALLA). *Journal of Multilingual and Multicultural Development, 9*, 43–58.

O'Malley, J. M., & Pierce, L. V. (1996). *Authentic assessment for English language learners: Practical approaches for teachers.* New York: Addison-Wesley.

O'Neill, R. E., Horner, R. H., Albin, R. W., Sprague, J. R., Storey, K., & Newton, J. S. (1997). *Functional assessment interview for problem behavior: A practical handbook* (2nd ed.). Pacific Grove, CA: Brooks/Cole.

Ormrod, J. E. (2000). *Educational psychology: Developing learners* (3rd ed.). Upper Saddle River, NJ: Merrill.

Ortiz, A. A., Wilkinson, C. Y., Robertson-Courtney, P., & Kushner, M. I. (2006). Considerations in implementing intervention assistance teams to support English language learners. *Remedial and Special Education, 27*(1), 53–63.

Ovando, C. J., Collier, V. P., & Combs, M. C. (2003). *Bilingual & ESL classrooms: Teaching in multicultural contexts.* Boston: McGraw Hill.

Palincsar, A. S., & Brown, A. L. (1984). The reciprocal teaching of comprehension—fostering and comprehension-monitoring activities. *Cognition and Instruction, 1*, 117–175.

Patton, J., & Day-Vines, N. (2002). A curriculum and pedagogy for cultural competence: Knowledge, skills and dispositions needed to guide the training of special and general education teachers. Unpublished manuscript.

Peregoy, S. F., & Boyle, O. F. (2001). *Reading, writing, and learning in ESL* (3rd ed.). New York: Longman.

Polloway, E. A., Patton, J. R., & Serna, L. (2008). *Strategies for teaching learners with special needs* (9th ed.). Columbus, OH: Pearson-Merrill.

Reddy, S. S., Utley, C. A., Delquardi, J. C., Mortweet, S. L., Greenwood, C. R., & Bowman, C. (1999). Peer tutoring for health and safety. *Teaching Exceptional Children, 31*(3), 44–52.

Rhodes, W. C., & Tracy, J. L. (1978). *Emotionally disturbed and deviant children: New views and approaches.* Englewood Cliffs, NJ: Prentice-Hall.

Rieth, H., & Evertson, C. (1988). Variables related to the effective instruction of difficult-to-teach children. *Focus on Exceptional Children, 20*(5), 1–7.

Rosenshine, B., & Meister, C. (1994). Reciprocal teaching: a review of the research. *Review of Educational Research, 64*, 479–530.

Rueda, R., & Kim, S. (2001). Cultural and linguistic diversity as a theoretical framework for understanding multicultural learners with mild disabilities. In C. A. Utley & F. E. Obiakor (eds.), *Special education, multicultural education, and school reform: Components of quality education for learners with mild disabilities* (pp. 74–89). Springfield, IL: Charles C. Thomas.

Saenz, L., Fuchs, L. S., & Fuchs, D. (2005). Peer-assisted learning strategies for English language learners with learning disabilities. *Exceptional Children, 71*, 231–247.

Salend, S. J., & Garrick-Duhaney, L. M. (2005). Understanding and addressing the disproportionate representation of students of color in special education. *Intervention in School and Clinic, 40*, 213–221.

Salvia, J., & Ysseldyke, J. (2003). *Assessment in special education and remedial education*. Boston: Houghton Mifflin.

Shade, B. J., & New, C. A. (1993). Cultural influences on learning. In J. A. Banks & C. A. Banks (eds.), *Multicultural education: Issues and perspectives* (2nd ed., 317–331). Boston: Allyn & Bacon.

Sherman, J. G. (1992). Reflections on PSI: Good news and bad. *Journal of Applied Behavior Analysis, 25*(1), 59–64.

Skrtic, T. M., Harris, K. R., & Shriner, J. G. (2005). *Special education policy and practice: Accountability, instruction and social change.* Denver, CO: Love Publishing.

Smith, C. R. (1991). *LD: The interaction of learner, task, and setting* (2nd ed.). Boston: Allyn & Bacon.

Smith, T. E. C., Polloway, E., Patton, J. R., & Dowdy, C. A. (2004). *Teaching students with special needs in inclusive settings* (4th ed.). Boston: Pearson/Allyn & Bacon.

Sorrells, A. M., Webb-Johnson, G., & Townsend, B. L. (2004). Multicultural perspectives in special education: A call for responsibility in research, practice, and teacher preparation. In A. M. Sorrells, H. J. Rieth, & P. T. Sindelar (eds.), *Critical issues in special education: Access, diversity and accountability* (pp. 73–105). Boston: Pearson/Allyn & Bacon.

Speece, D. L., & Walker, C. Y. (2007). What are the issues in response to intervention research? In D. Hagger, J. Klingner, & S. Vaughn (eds.), *Evidence-based reading practices for response to intervention* (pp. 287–301). Baltimore, MD: Paul H. Brookes.

Stefanakis, E. H. (1998). *Whose judgment counts: Assessing bilingual children K–3.* Portsmouth, NH: Heinemann.

Tharp, R. G. (1997). *From at-risk to excellence: Research, theory and principles for practice.* Santa Cruz, CA: Center for Research on Education, Diversity and Excellence (CREDE).

The Teaching Commission. (2004). *Teaching at risk: A call to action.* New York, NY: Author.

Thomas, W. P. (1992). *County of Arlington (VA) ESEA title VII program: The Cognitive Academic Language Learning Approach (CALLA) project for mathematics, 1991–1992.* Evaluation report submitted to the Office of Bilingual Education, U.S. Department of Education.

Thomas, G., & Pring, R. (2004). *Evidence-based practice in education.* New York: Open University Press.

U.S. Department of Education. (2002). *The facts about investigating in what works.* Washington, DC: Author. (Cited April 15, 2007). www.ed.gov/nclb/methods/whatworks/whatworks.html

U.S. Department of Education, National Center for Education Statistics, "The Nation's Report Card: Reading Highlights 2003," 2003a. Washington, DC.

U.S. Department of Education, National Center for Education Statistics, "The Nation's Report Card: Mathematics Highlights 2003," 2003b. Washington, DC.

Vaidero, D. (2000). Lags in minority achievement defy traditional explanations. *Education Week, 19*(28), 1, 18–22.

Vaughn, S., Cirino, P. T., Linan-Thompson, S., Mathes, P. G., Carlson, C. D., Hagan, E. C., Pollard-Durodola, S. D., Fletcher, J. M., & Francis, D. J. (2006). Effectiveness of a Spanish intervention and an English intervention for English-language learners at risk for reading problems. *American Educational Research Journal, 43*(3), 449–487.

Vaughn, S. (2003). How many tiers are needed for response to intervention to achieve acceptable prevention outcomes? Paper presented at the National Research Center on Learning Disabilities Responsiveness-to-Interventions Symposium, Kansas City, MO.

Vaughn, S., Linan-Thompson, S., & Hickman, P. (2003). Response to instruction as a means of identifying students with reading/learning disabilities. *Exceptional Children, 69*(4), 391–409.

Vaughn, S., & Fuchs, D. (2003). Redefining learning disabilities as inadequate response to instruction: The promise and potential problems. *Learning Disabilities: Research & Practice, 18*(3), 137–146.

Viadero, D. (March 2000). Lags in Minority Achievement Defy Traditional Explanations, *Education Week, 19*(28), 1, 18–22.

Walther-Thomas, C., Korinek, L., & McLaughlin, V. L. (2005). Collaboration to support student's success. In T. M. Skrtic, K. R. Harris, & J. G. Shriner (eds.), *Special education policy and practice: Accountability, instruction and social challenges* (pp. 182–211). Denver, CO: Love Publishing.

Webber, J., & Plotts, C. A. (2008). *Emotional and behavioral disorders: Theory and practice.* Boston: Allyn & Bacon.

Weber, J., & Scheuermann, B. (1991). Accentuate the positive . . . . Eliminate the negative! *Teaching Exceptional Children, 24,* 14–17.

What Works Clearinghouse. www.whatworks.ed.gov. Accessed May 1, 2007.

Wiley, T. G. (1996). Literacy and language diversity in sociocultural contexts. *Literacy and language diversity in the United States.* Washington, DC: Center for Applied Linguistics and Delta Systems.

Wilkinson, C. Y., Ortiz, A., & Robertson-Courtney, P. (2004). Appropriate eligibility determination for English language learners suspected of having reading-related learning disabilities—Linking school history, prereferral, referral and assessment data. Paper presented at the 2004 *NCCRESt Conference, English Language Learners Struggling to Learn: Emergent Research on Linguistic Differences and Learning Disabilities,* Tempe, AZ.

Winzer, M. A., & Mazurek, K. (1998). *Special education in multicultural contexts.* Columbus, OH: Merrill.

Woolfolk, A. E. (2006). *Educational psychology.* Englewood Cliffs, NJ: Prentice-Hall.

Wright, J. (2007). RTI Toolkit: *A practical guide for schools.* Port Chester, NY: Dude Publishing.

Yates, J. R., & Ortiz, A. A. (2004). Classification issues in special education for English language learners. In A. M. Sorrells, H. J. Rieth, & P. T. Sindelar (eds.), *Critical issues in special education: Access, diversity, and accountability* (pp. 38–56). Boston: Pearson.

Yell, M. (2004). Understanding the three-tier model. Presentation at the Colorado State Directors of Special Education Meeting, Denver, CO.